DOING YOUR RESEARCH PROJECT

A guide for first-time researchers
in education and social science

Third edition

JUDITH BELL

Open University Press
Buckingham · Philadelphia

Open University Press
Celtic Court
22 Ballmoor
Buckingham MK18 1XW

email:enquiries@openup.co.uk
world wide web: www.openup.co.uk

and
325 Chestnut Street
Philadelphia, PA 19106, USA

First edition published 1987
Reprinted 1988, 1989 (twice), 1991, 1992 (twice)

First published in the second edition 1993
Reprinted 1993, 1995, 1996, 1997, 1998, 1999

First published in this third edition 1999
Reprinted 2000, 2001, 2002

A catalogue record of this book is available from the British Library

ISBN 0 335 20388 4 (pb)   0 335 20389 2 (hb)

Library of Congress Cataloging-in-Publication Data
Bell, Judith, 1930–
    Doing your research project: a guide for first-time researchers
in education and social science/Judith Bell. – 3rd ed.   p.   cm.
    ISBN 0-335-20389-2 (hardcover). – ISBN 0-335-20388-4 (pbk.)
    Includes bibliographical references and index.
    1. Education–Research.   2. Education–Research–Methodology.
3. Social sciences–Research.   4. Social sciences–Research–
Methodology.   5. Independent study.   I. Title.
LB1028.B394   1999
370'.7'2–dc21   99–17596   CIP

Typeset by Type Study, Scarborough, North Yorkshire
Printed in Great Britain by St Edmundsbury Press Ltd, Bury St Edmunds,
Suffolk

DOING YOUR RESEARCH PROJECT

Third edition

CONTENTS

3 Negotiating access, ethics and the problems of 'inside' research   37

4 Keeping records, making notes and locating libraries   48

5 Finding and searching information sources   64
Sally Baker

PREFACE TO THE THIRD EDITION

The first edition of this book was written as a result of the accumulated experience of teaching research methods to postgraduate students in British and overseas universities and of writing distance learning materials for the Open University and the University of Sheffield. There are many good books on research methods on the market, but at that time, I had been unable to find one which quite covered the basic principles involved in planning research which was written in plain English and which made no assumptions about students' previous knowledge of research. *Doing Your Research Project* was intended to be a confidence builder and to provide new researchers with the skills and techniques to enable them to move on to more complex tasks and reading. I am told it is now a set book for many undergraduate and postgraduate courses.

All the techniques and procedures described in the first edition were well tried and tested, but there are always ways of doing things better. The experience of working through some of the procedures in research methods workshops in some cases suggested alternative approaches and the desirability of providing additional material. These were incorporated into the second edition in 1993, including a new chapter on interpretation and presentation of the evidence.

Further changes have become necessary for this third edition.

When the first edition was published, relatively few students were skilled in information technology (IT) and only the most advanced libraries provided general access to computer search facilities. Now, times have changed so it has become necessary to provide new material on access to libraries, search techniques, locating published materials, computer databases and the Internet. Much good research is done without access to complex equipment, but if the facilities are there to make our lives easier, it is only sensible to make use of them.

Other changes in this edition include enlarged chapters on approaches to educational research and on the analysis of documentary evidence; additions to several other chapters; updating of the suggestions for additional reading and adjustments and additions to checklists. However, the basic structure remains the same as in the first and second editions. Feedback from students and from teachers has indicated that it has worked well over the years, and I hope you will continue to find the format and content useful.

Judith Bell

ACKNOWLEDGEMENTS

I have been helped throughout the preparation of all three editions of this book by the interest of colleagues and friends who were once first-time researchers themselves but are now expert practitioners. I have particularly welcomed guidance from research students who kindly (and sometimes gleefully) pointed out that they had found better ways of doing things than I suggested in the first two editions. I have been happy to incorporate all their suggestions.

My thanks to Brendan Duffy and Stephen Waters, two outstanding former Open University research students who carried out investigations into aspects of educational management in their own institutions and developed a considerable degree of expertise in research methods in the process. Both generously allowed me to use some of their ideas and experiences. Brendan, who already held a PhD in history before he embarked on research into education management, wrote 'The analysis of documentary evidence' in the first two editions and has extended and updated the original versions for this edition.

I am grateful to Alan Woodley, Senior Research Fellow at the Open University for permission to continue to draw on his literature review in Chapter 6 and to Clara Nai, Singaporean-based former postgraduate student of the University of Sheffield, for permitting me to quote parts of her MEd literature review, also in Chapter 6. My particular thanks to Jan Gray and to Sally Baker for providing new material for this third edition. Jan, holder of a prestigious university prize for research, recently completed her doctoral study at the Edith Cowan University in Western Australia. She contributed the section on narrative inquiry in Chapter 1 and her enthusiasm for this approach not only encouraged me to read further but also to begin to understand what is involved in narrative research.

Sally Baker, Education and Social Sciences librarian at the Open University library was persuaded to write Chapter 5, and managed to guide us expertly through the highways and byways of computer databases, literature searching and managing information, without blinding us all with technology. I have learnt a great deal by working with both Jan and Sally.

Finally, to all of you who once again painstakingly read drafts, sometimes at short notice, provided comments, offered advice or drew attention to errors and omissions, as always, my grateful thanks.

INTRODUCTION

This book is intended for those of you who are about to undertake some sort of educational research in connection with your job, or as a requirement for an undergraduate, diploma or postgraduate course.

If you are a beginner researcher, the problems facing you are much the same whether you are producing a small project, an MEd dissertation or a PhD thesis. You will need to select a topic, identify the objectives of your study, plan and design a suitable methodology, devise research instruments, negotiate access to institutions, materials and people, collect, analyse and present information and finally, produce a well-written report or dissertation. Whatever the size of the undertaking, techniques have to be mastered and a plan of action devised which does not attempt more than the limitations of expertise, time and access permit. Large-scale research projects will require sophisticated techniques and, often, statistical and computational expertise, but it is quite possible to produce a worthwhile study without using computers and with a minimum of statistical knowledge.

We all learn how to do research by actually doing it, but a great deal of time can be wasted and goodwill dissipated by inadequate preparation. This book aims to provide you with the tools to do the job, to help you to avoid some of the pitfalls and time-wasting false trails that can eat into your time allowance, to establish good research habits and to take you from the stage of selecting a topic through to the production of a well-planned, methodologically sound and well-written final report or dissertation – ON TIME. There is, after all, little point in doing all the work if you never manage to submit.

Throughout this book, I use the terms 'research', 'investigation', 'inquiry' and 'study' interchangeably, though I realize this is not acceptable to everyone.

Some argue that 'research' is a more rigorous and technically more complicated form of investigation. Howard and Sharp discuss this issue in *The Management of a Student Research Project*:

> Most people associate the word 'research' with activities which are substantially removed from day-to-day life and which are pursued by outstandingly gifted persons with an unusual level of commitment. There is of course a good deal of truth in this viewpoint, but we would argue that the pursuit is not restricted to this type of person and indeed can prove to be a stimulating and satisfying experience for many people with a trained and enquiring mind.
>
> (Howard and Sharp 1983: 6)

They define research (p. 6) as 'seeking through methodical processes to add to one's own body of knowledge and, hopefully, to that of others, by the discovery of non-trivial facts and insights'.

Drew (1980) agrees that 'research is conducted to solve problems and to expand knowledge' (p. 4) and stresses that 'research is a systematic way of asking questions, a systematic method of enquiry' (p. 8). It is the *systematic* approach that is important in the conduct of your projects, not the title of 'research', 'investigation', 'inquiry' or 'study'. Where collection of data is involved (notes of interviews, questionnaire responses, articles, official reports, minutes of meetings, etc.), orderly record-keeping and thorough planning are essential.

No book can take the place of a good supervisor, but good supervisors are in great demand, and if you can familiarize yourself with basic approaches and techniques, you will be able to make full use of your tutorial time for priority issues.

The examples given in the following chapters relate particularly to projects which have to be completed in two to three months (what I have called the '100-hour' projects), but I have been pleased to learn that numbers of MEd, MPhil and PhD students have found them equally useful. I hope you do too.

 **Part I**

PREPARING THE GROUND

1

APPROACHES TO EDUCATIONAL RESEARCH

It is perfectly possible to carry out a worthwhile investigation without having detailed knowledge of the various approaches to or styles of educational research, but a study of different approaches will give insight into different ways of planning an investigation, and, incidentally, will also enhance your understanding of the literature. One of the problems of reading about research methods and reading research reports is the terminology. Researchers use terms and occasionally jargon that may be incomprehensible to other people. It is the same in any field, where a specialized language develops to ease communication among professionals. So, before considering the various stages of planning and conducting investigations, it may be helpful to consider the main features of certain well-established and well-reported styles of research.

Different styles, traditions or approaches use different methods of collecting data, but no approach prescribes nor automatically rejects any particular method. Quantitative researchers collect facts and study the relationship of one set of facts to another. They use techniques that are likely to produce quantified and, if possible, generalizable conclusions. Researchers adopting a qualitative perspective are more concerned to understand individuals' perceptions of the world. They seek insight rather than statistical analysis. They doubt whether social 'facts' exist and question whether a 'scientific' approach can be used when dealing with human beings. Yet there are occasions when qualitative researchers draw on quantitative techniques, and *vice versa*.

Classifying an approach as quantitative or qualitative, ethnographic, survey, action research or whatever, does not mean that once an approach has been selected, the researcher may not move from the methods normally associated with that style. Each approach has its strengths and weaknesses and each is particularly suitable for a particular context. The approach adopted and the methods of data collection selected will depend on the nature of the inquiry and the type of information required.

It is impossible in the space of a few pages to do justice to any of the well-established styles of research, but the following will at least provide a basis for further reading and may give you ideas about approaches which you may wish to adopt in your own investigation.

Action research and the 'teacher as researcher' model

There are many definitions of action research. Cohen and Manion describe it as

> essentially an on-the-spot procedure designed to deal with a concrete problem located in an immediate situation. This means that ideally, the step-by-step process is constantly monitored over varying periods of time and by a variety of mechanisms (questionnaires, diaries, interviews and case studies, for example) so that the ensuing feedback may be translated into modifications, adjustments, directional changes, redefinitions, as necessary, so as to bring about lasting benefit to the ongoing process itself rather than to some future occasion . . .
>
> (Cohen and Manion 1994: 192)

As they point out, an important feature of action research is that the task is not finished when the project ends. The participants continue to review, evaluate and improve practice. Elliott (1991: 69) takes the definition a stage further:

It aims to feed practical judgement in concrete situations, and the validity of the 'theories' or hypotheses it generates depends not so much on 'scientific' tests of truth, as on their usefulness in helping people to act more intelligently and skilfully. In action research 'theories' are not validated independently and then applied to practice. They are validated through practice.

Brown and McIntyre, who describe an action-research model for curriculum innovation in Scottish schools, also draw attention to the principle of deriving hypotheses from practice. They write:

> The research questions arise from an analysis of the problems of the practitioners in the situation and the immediate aim then becomes that of understanding those problems. The researcher/actor, at an early stage, formulates speculative, tentative, general principles in relation to the problems that have been identified; from these principles, hypotheses may then be generated about what action is likely to lead to the desired improvements in practice. Such action will then be tried out and data on its effects collected; these data are used to revise the earlier hypotheses and identify more appropriate action that reflects a modification of the general principles. Collection of data on the effects of this new action may then generate further hypotheses and modified principles, and so on as we move towards a greater understanding and improvement of practice. This implies a continuous process of research and the worth of the work is judged by the understanding of, and desirable change in, the practice that is achieved.
>
> (Brown and McIntyre 1981: 245)

The essentially practical, problem-solving nature of action research makes this approach attractive to practitioner-researchers who have identified a problem during the course of their work and see the merit of investigating it and, if possible, of improving practice. There is nothing new about practitioners operating as researchers, and the 'teacher as researcher' model has been extensively discussed (Bartholomew 1971, Cope and Gray 1979, Raven and Parker 1981).

Action research is not, of course, limited to projects carried out by teachers in an educational setting. It is appropriate in any context when 'specific knowledge is required for a specific problem in a specific situation, or when a new approach is to be grafted on to an existing system' (Cohen and Manion 1994: 194). Action research needs to be planned in the same systematic way as any other type of research, and the methods selected for gathering information will depend on the nature of the information required. Action research is not a method or technique. It is an approach which has proved to be particularly attractive to educators because of its practical, problem-solving emphasis, because practitioners (sometimes with researchers from outside the institution; other times not) carry out the research and because the research is directed towards greater understanding and improvement of practice *over a period of time.*

Case study

The case-study approach is particularly appropriate for individual researchers because it gives an opportunity for one aspect of a problem to be studied in some depth within a limited time scale (though some case studies are carried out over a long period of time, as with Elizabeth Richardson's (1973) three-year study of Nailsea School).

Case study has been described as 'an umbrella term for a family of research methods having in common the decision to focus on inquiry around an instance' (Adelman *et al.* 1977). It is much more than a story about or a description of an event or state. As in all research, evidence is collected systematically, the relationship between variables is studied and the study is methodically planned. Case study is concerned principally with the interaction of factors and events and, as Nisbet and Watt (1980: 5) point out, 'sometimes it is only by taking a practical instance that we can obtain a full picture of this interaction'. Though observation and interviews are most frequently used in case study, no method is excluded. Methods of collecting information are selected which are appropriate for the task.

The great strength of the case-study method is that is allows the researcher to concentrate on a specific instance or situation and to identify, or attempt to identify, the various interactive processes at work. These processes may remain hidden in a large-scale survey but may be crucial to the success or failure of systems or organizations.

Case studies may be carried out to follow up and to put flesh on the bones of a survey. They can precede a survey and be used as a means of identifying key issues which merit further investigation, but the majority of case studies are carried out as free-standing exercises. The researcher identifies an 'instance', which could be the introduction of a new syllabus, the way a school adapts to a new role, or any innovation or stage of development in an institution – and observes, questions, studies. Each organization has its common and its unique features. The case-study researcher aims to identify such features and to show how they affect the implementation of systems and influence the way an organization functions.

Inevitably, where a single researcher is gathering all the information, selection has to be made. The researcher selects the area for study and decides which material to present in the final report. It is difficult to cross-check information and so there is always the danger of distortion. Critics of the case-study approach draw attention to this and other problems. They point to the fact that generalization is not always possible, and question the value of the study of single events. Others disagree.

Denscombe (1998: 36–7) makes the point that 'the extent to which findings from the case study can be generalized to other examples in the class depends on how far the case study example is similar to others of its type', and, drawing on the example of a case study of a small primary school, cautions that

> this means that the researcher must obtain data on the significant features (catchment area, the ethnic origins of the pupils and the amount of staff turnover) for primary schools in general, and then demonstrate where the case study example fits in relation to the overall picture.
>
> (p. 37)

Bassey holds similar views, but prefers to use the term 'relatability' rather than 'generalizability'. In his opinion, an important criterion for judging the merit of a case study is the extent to which the details are sufficient and appropriate for a teacher working in a similar situation to relate his decision making to that described in the case study. The relatability of a case study is more important than its generalisability.

(Bassey 1981: 85)

He considers that if case studies

are carried out systematically and critically, if they are aimed at the improvement of education, if they are relatable, and if by publication of the findings they extend the boundaries of existing knowledge, then they are valid forms of educational research.

(p. 86)

A successful study will provide the reader with a three-dimensional picture and will illustrate relationships, micropolitical issues and patterns of influences in a particular context.

A word of warning. Single researchers working to a deadline and within a limited timescale need to be very careful about the selection of case study topic. As Yin (1994: 137) reminds us:

Case studies have been done about decisions, about programmes, about the implementation process, and about organizational change. Beware these types of topic – none is easily defined in terms of the beginning or end point of the 'case'.

He considers that 'the more a study contains specific propositions, the more it will stay within reasonable limits' (p. 137). And we all have to keep our research within reasonable limits, regardless of whether we are working on a 100-hour project or a PhD.

The ethnographic style

The ethnographic style of fieldwork research was developed originally by anthropologists who wished to study a society or some aspect of a society, culture or group in depth. They developed an approach which depended heavily on observation and, in some cases, complete or partial integration into the society being studied. This form of participant observation enabled the researchers, as far as was possible, to share the same experiences as the subjects, to understand better why they acted in the way they did and 'to see things as those involved see things' (Denscombe 1998: 69). This approach is no longer limited to anthropological studies and has been effectively used in a good many studies of small groups.

Participant observation takes time and so is often outside the scope of researchers working on 100-hour projects. The researcher has to be accepted by the individuals or groups being studied, and this can mean doing the same job, or living in the same environment and circumstances as the subjects for lengthy periods. Time is not the only problem with this approach. As in case studies, critics point to the problem of representativeness. If the researcher is studying one group in depth over a period of time, who is to say that group is typical of other groups which may have the same title? Are teachers in one school necessarily representative of teachers in a similar school in another part of the country? Are canteen workers in one type of organization likely to be typical of all canteen workers? Generalizability may be a problem, but as in the case-study approach the study may be relatable in a way that will enable members of similar groups to recognize problems and, possibly, to see ways of solving similar problems in their own group.

Surveys

The aim of a survey is to obtain information which can be analysed and patterns extracted and comparisons made. The census is one example of a survey in which the same questions are asked of the selected population (the population being the group or category of individuals selected). The census aims to cover 100 per cent of the population, but most surveys have less ambitious aims. In most cases, a survey will aim to obtain information from a representative selection of the population and from that sample will then be able to present the findings as being representative of the population as a whole. Inevitably, there are problems in the survey method. Great care has to be taken to ensure that the sample population is truly representative. At a very simple level, that means ensuring that if the total population has 1000 men and 50 women, then the same proportion of men to women has to be selected. But that example grossly oversimplifies the method of drawing a representative sample, and if you decide to carry out a survey, you will need to consider what characteristics of the total population need to be represented in your sample to enable you to say with fair confidence that your sample is reasonably representative.

In surveys, all respondents will be asked the same questions in, as far as possible, the same circumstances. Question wording is not as easy as it seems, and careful piloting is necessary to ensure that all questions mean the same to all respondents. Information can be gathered by means of self-completion questionnaires (as in the case of the census) or by means of questionnaires, schedules or checklists administered by an interviewer. Whichever method of information gathering is selected, the aim is to obtain answers to the same questions from a large number of individuals to enable the researcher not only to describe but also to compare, to relate one characteristic to another and to demonstrate that certain features exist in certain categories. Surveys can provide answers to the questions What? Where? When? and How?, but it is not so easy to find out Why? Causal relationships can rarely if ever be proved by survey method. The main emphasis is on fact-finding, and if a survey is well structured and piloted, it can be a relatively cheap and quick way of obtaining information.

The experimental style

It is relatively easy to plan experiments which deal with measurable phenomena. For example, experiments have been set up to measure the effects of using fluoridated toothpaste on dental caries by establishing a control group (who did not use the toothpaste) and an experimental group (who did). In such experiments, the two groups, matched for age, sex, ratio of boys to girls, social class and so on were given a pre-test dental examination and instructions about which toothpaste to use. After a year, both groups were given the post-test dental examination and conclusions were then drawn about the effectiveness or otherwise of the fluoridated toothpaste. The principle of such experiments is that if two identical groups are selected, one of which (the experimental group) is given special treatment and the other (the control group) is not, then any differences between the two groups at the end of the experimental period may be attributed to the difference in treatment. A causal relationship has been established. It may be fairly straightforward to test the extent of dental caries (though even in this experiment the extent of the caries could be caused by many factors not controlled by the experiment), but it is quite another matter to test changes in behaviour. As Wilson (1979) points out, social causes do not work singly. Any examination of low school attainment or high IQ is the product of multiple causes:

> To isolate each cause requires a new experimental group each time and the length and difficulty of the experiment increases rapidly. It is possible to run an experiment in which several treatments are put into practice simultaneously but many groups must be made available rather than just two . . . The causes of social phenomena are usually multiple ones and an experiment to study them requires large numbers of people often for lengthy periods. This requirement limits the usefulness of the experimental method.
>
> (Wilson 1979: 22)

So, the experimental style does allow conclusions to be drawn about cause and effect, if the experimental design is sound, but in education and the social sciences generally, large groups are needed if the many variations and ambiguities involved in human behaviour are to be controlled. Such large-scale experiments are expensive to set up and take more time than most students working on 100-hour projects can give. Some tests which require only a few hours (e.g. to test short-term memory or perception) can be very effective, but in claiming a causal relationship, great care needs to be taken to ensure that all possible causes have been considered.

Narrative inquiry

It is only recently that I have become interested in the use and interpretation of narratives and in particular the acceptance of stories as valuable sources of data. Stories are certainly interesting and have been used for many years by management consultants and others who present examples of successful (and unsuccessful) practice as a basis for discussion as to how successful practice might be emulated and disasters avoided. What has always taxed me has been how information derived from storytelling can be structured in such a way as to produce valid research findings. It took an experienced group of postgraduate and postdoctoral students who had planned their research on narrative inquiry lines to sort me out and to explain precisely what was involved. I was not even sure what 'narrative inquiry' actually meant and so, always believing the best way to find out is to ask an expert, I asked one member of the group, Dr Janette Gray, to tell me. She wrote as follows:

> It involves the collection and development of stories, either as a form of data collection or as a means of structuring a research project. Informants often speak in a story form during the interviews, and as the researcher, listening and attempting to understand, we hear their 'stories'. The research method can be described as narrative when data collection, interpretation and writing are considered a 'meaning-making' process with similar characteristics to stories (Gudmunsdottir 1996: 295). Narrative inquiry can involve reflective autobiography, life story, or the inclusion of excerpts from participants' stories to illustrate a theme developed by the researcher. A narrative approach to inquiry is most appropriate when the researcher is interested in portraying intensely personal accounts of human experience. Narratives allow voice – to the researcher, the participants and to cultural groups – and in this sense they can have the ability to develop a decidely political and powerful edge.
>
> (Gray 1998: 1)

Colleagues to whom I had earlier spoken and who had successfully adopted a narrative inquiry approach to one or more of their research projects had always made it clear that stories were not used merely as a series of 'story boxes' piled on top of one another and with no particular structure or connecting theme. The problem I had was in understanding how such structures and themes could be derived. Jan's explanation was as follows:

> All forms of narrative inquiry involve an element of analysis and development of themes, dependent on the researcher's perspective. Stories share a basic structure. The power of a story is dependent on the storyteller's use of language to present an interpretation of personal experience. The skill of the narrative researcher lies in the ability to structure the interview data into a form which clearly presents a sense of a beginning, middle and an end. Even though the use of story as a research tool is a relatively new concept in the social sciences, historically story has been an accepted way of relating knowledge and developing self-knowledge. One of the major strengths of such a means of conducting inquiry is the ability to allow readers who do not share a cultural background similar to either the storyteller or the researcher to develop an understanding of motives and consequences of actions described within a story format. Narrative is a powerful and different way of knowing . . .
>
> Data collection for narrative research requires the researcher to allow the storyteller to structure the conversations, with the researcher asking follow-up questions. So a narrative approach to the question of how mature-age undergraduates perceive their ability to cope with the experience of returning to study would involve extended, open-ended interviews with one or two mature-aged students. This would allow the students to express their personal experience of the problems, frustrations and joys of returning to study. It might also involve similar 'conversations' with other stakeholders in their education – perhaps family members; their tutors and lecturers – to provide a multiple perspective of the context of the education of mature-aged undergraduates.
>
> (Gray 1998: 2)

Jan added that 'the benefit of considerate and careful negotiation will be a story allowing an incredibly personal and multi-faceted insight into the situation being discussed'. I am sure this is so. I have become convinced of the value of this approach and that stories can in some cases serve to enhance understanding within a case study or an ethnographic study. However, narratives can present their own set of problems:

> Interviews are time-consuming and require the researcher to allow the storytellers to recount in their own way the experience of being (or teaching) a student. This may not emerge in the first interview. Until a trust relationship has developed between researcher and storyteller, it is highly unlikely that such intimate information will be shared. Such personal involvement with the researcher involves risks and particular ethical issues. The storytellers may decide they have revealed more of their feelings than they are prepared to share publicly and they may insist either on substantial editing or on withdrawing from the project.
>
> (Gray 1998: 2)

Problems of this kind can arise in almost any kind of research, particularly those which are heavily dependent on interview data, but the close relationship needed for narrative inquiry can make the researcher (and the storyteller) particularly vulnerable.

The fact that the narrative approach carries with it numbers of potential difficulties, particularly for first-time researchers, and researchers operating within a particularly tight schedule, certainly does not mean that it should be disregarded when considering an appropriate approach to the topic of your choice. Far from it – but as is the case with all research planning, I feel it would be as well to discuss the issues fully with your supervisor before deciding what to do, and if possible to try to find a supervisor who is experienced, or at least interested in narrative inquiry.

Which approach?

Classifying an approach as ethnographic, qualitative, experimental, or whatever, does not mean that once an approach has been selected, the researcher may not move from the methods normally associated with that style. But understanding the major advantages and disadvantages of each approach is likely to help you to select the most appropriate methodology for the task in hand. This chapter covers only the very basic principles associated with the different styles or approaches to research which will suffice – at any rate until you have decided on a topic and considered what information you need to obtain.

Further reading is provided at the end of this chapter. As far as possible, I have tried to indicate books and journals which should be available in academic libraries. However, always consult the library catalogue. If there is an on-line facility, the librarian will show you how the system operates. Then take advantage of what the library has in stock or is able to obtain from another library in the area – preferably without cost. Borrowing books through the interlibrary loan system can be quite expensive – and it can be slow.

Further reading

Adelman, C., Jenkins, D. and Kemmis, S. (1977) 'Re-thinking case study: notes from the second Cambridge conference', *Cambridge Journal of Education*, 6, 139–50. Also reproduced as Chapter 6 in Bell, J. *et al.* (1984) *Conducting Small-scale Investigations in Educational Management*. London: Paul Chapman.

Atkinson, P. and Delamont, S. (1985) 'A critique of "case study" research in education' in Shipman, M. (ed.) *Educational Research: Principles, Policies and Practices*. Lewes: Falmer Press.

Bassey, M. (1981) 'Pedagogic research: on the relative merits of search for generalisation and study of single events', *Oxford Review of Education*, 7(1), 73–93. Also reproduced as Chapter 7 in Bell, J. *et al.* (1984).

Bogdan, R.C. and Biklen, S.K. (1982) *Qualitative Research for Education: An Introduction to Theory and Methods*. Boston, MA: Allyn & Bacon.

Bromley, D.B. (1986) *The Case Study Method in Psychology and Related Disciplines*. Chichester: John Wiley.

Carr, W. and Kemmis, S. (1986) *Becoming Critical: Education, Knowledge and Action Research*. Lewes: Falmer Press.

Casey, K. (1993) 'The new narrative research in education', *Review of Research in Education*, 21, 211–53.

Cohen, L. and Manion, L. (1994) 'Case studies', Chapter 5 in *Research Methods in Education*, 4th edn. London: Routledge.

Denscombe, M. (1998) *The Good Research Guide*. Buckingham: Open

University Press. Chapter 2, pp. 30–41 provides a clear account of the advantages and limitations of case study. Chapter 3 deals with experiments, Chapter 4 with action research and Chapter 5 with ethnography.

Elliott, J. (1991) *Action Research for Educational Change*. Buckingham: Open University Press.

Hammersley, M. (1990) *Classroom Ethnography: Empirical and Methodological Essays*. Buckingham: Open University Press.

Hammersley, M. and Atkinson, P. (1983) *Ethnography: Principles in Practice*. London: Tavistock.

Hart, E. and Bond, M. (1995) *Action Research for Health and Social Care*. Buckingham: Open University Press.

Marsh, C. (1982) *The Survey Method: The Contribution of Surveys to Sociological Explanation*. London: Allen & Unwin.

McNiff, J. (1988) *Action Research: Principles and Practice*. Basingstoke: Macmillan Education.

Moser, C.A. and Kalton, G. (1971) *Survey Methods in Social Investigation*, 2nd edn. London: Heinemann.

Nisbet, J. and Watt, J. (1980) *Case Study*. Rediguide 26. University of Nottingham, School of Education. Also reproduced as Chapter 5 in Bell, J. *et al*. (1984).

Thody, A. with Downes, P., Hewlett, M. and Tomlinson, H. (1997) 'Lies, damned lies – and storytelling: an exploration of the contribution of principals' anecdotes to research, teaching and learning about the management of schools and colleges, *Educational Management and Administration*, 25, 3, July.

Wilson, N.J. (1979) 'The ethnographic style of research' in Block 1 (Variety in Social Science Research), Part I (Styles of Research) of Open University course DE304, *Research Methods in Education and the Social Sciences*. Milton Keynes: Open University Educational Enterprises. Also reproduced as Chapter 2 in Bell, J. *et al*. (1984).

Winter, R. (1987) *Action Research and the Nature of Social Inquiry: Professional Innovation and Educational Work*. Aldershot: Avebury.

2

PLANNING THE PROJECT

Selecting a topic

You may be given a topic to research, in which case the decision is already taken for you, but in most cases you will be asked to select a topic from a list or to decide on a topic yourself. You may have an idea or a particular area of interest that you would like to explore. You may have several ideas, all equally interesting. If so, write them down: *mature students in higher education; appraisal; stress among senior managers; something to do with in-service training.* All good topics, but before a decision is made about which to select, some work needs to be done. You will not have time to read extensively on each topic, but consult the library catalogue to see how much has been written, inquire in the library about dissertations and articles which may have been written on similar topics and talk to your colleagues and fellow students. Talking through problems and possible topics with colleagues is an essential stage of any plan. Their views may differ from or even conflict with your own and may suggest alternative lines of inquiry. They may be aware of sensitive aspects of certain topics which could cause difficulties at some stage or know of recent publications which are not listed in the library catalogue. If you are hoping to carry out your research in your own institution, then another very good reason for discussing possible topics with colleagues is that you will probably be asking for their support and collaboration: early consultation is essential if you are to avoid difficulties later.

Selecting a topic is more difficult than it seems at first. With limited time at your disposal there is a temptation to select a topic before the ground work has been done, but try to resist the temptation. Prepare the ground work well and you will save time later. Your discussions and inquiries will help you to select a topic which is likely to be of interest, which you have a good chance of completing, which will be worth the effort and which may even have some practical application later on.

Many educational researchers stress the desirability of considering the practical outcomes of research. Langeveld makes the point that

> Educational studies . . . are a 'practical science' in the sense that we do not only want to know facts and to understand relations for the sake of knowledge, we want to know and understand in order to be able to act and act 'better' than we did before.
>
> (Langeveld 1965: 4)

This is not to deny the importance of educational research that may not have an immediate practical outcome. Eggleston provides a timely reminder of the importance of longer-term objectives and of the need to look beyond current educational practices. To restrict educational research to current educational practices would, in his opinion, lay it 'open to the charge that its sole function was to increase the efficiency of the existing system in terms of accepted criteria and deny it the opportunity to explore potentially more effective alternatives' (Eggleston 1979: 5).

Clearly the need for exploring potentially more effective alternatives to the present educational provision will always exist. After 100 hours of study, you are unlikely to be in a position to make recommendations for fundamental change in the educational system. However, whatever the size and scope of the study, you will in all cases analyse and evaluate the information you collect and you may then be in a position to suggest action which will bring about changes in policy and/or improvements in practice.

Discuss possible practical outcomes with your supervisor and decide what the emphasis of your study is to be. Is applicability to be important or is your study to have different aims? Once you have decided on a topic, the precise focus of the study needs to be established. You will need to decide exactly which aspects of your topic are to be investigated and to consider the questions you would like to ask.

The 'first thoughts' list and establishing the focus of the study

In a short project it is not possible to do everything, so consider your priorities. If you have decided that you would be interested in investigating barriers to learning among mature undergraduates, for example, draw up a 'first thoughts' list of questions. At this stage, the order and wording are not important. Your aim is to write down all possible questions, no matter how vague. You will refine and order them later on. Your list might be on the following lines:

1   What is meant by 'mature' in the context of this investigation?
2   Is there any relationship between subject/faculty and performance?
3   Are there any differences between the performance of mature students and students who start a degree course straight from school?
4   Do mature students who embark on a degree course without A levels do better or worse than mature students who have A levels?
5   What barriers to learning do mature students themselves identify?
6   What barriers to learning do their lecturers/tutors identify? Are they the same?
7   What do mature students feel would enhance their learning/help them to overcome any barriers to learning?
8   Do mature students experience any barriers to learning which are different from those experienced by younger students? If so, what?

9   Which tutoring/presentation styles have mature students found particularly helpful (or the reverse)?

10 If mature students had the opportunity to plan an induction and support system, what form would it take?

At this point, you may realize that it will be necessary to refine some of the questions. Ask yourself precisely what you mean by each one. Are you sure the vocabulary you have used is likely to mean the same to students and lecturers as it does to you? You will probably find that some questions can be broken down into several smaller items. As you subject yourself to rigorous examination of each question, you will begin to clarify what the aims and objectives of your study are and to establish the focus of the study.

Each stage is a process of refining and clarifying so that you end with a list of questions, tasks or objectives which you can ask, perform or examine. Decide exactly what it is you are trying to find out and why. Asking why you need certain information will help you to eliminate irrelevant items and will focus your attention on important aspects of the topic.

Hypothesis or objectives?

Many research projects begin with the statement of a hypothesis, defined by Verma and Beard as

> a tentative proposition which is subject to verification through subsequent investigation. It may also be seen as the guide to the researcher in that it depicts and describes the method to be followed in studying the problem. In many cases hypotheses are hunches that the researcher has about the existence of relationship between variables.
>
> (Verma and Beard 1981: 184)

This definition is taken a step further by Medawar, who writes

> All advances in scientific understanding, at every level, begin with a speculative adventure, an imaginative preconception *of what might be true* – a preconception which always, and

necessarily, goes a little way (sometimes a long way) beyond anything which we have logical or factual authority to believe in. It is the invention of a possible world, or of a tiny fraction of that world. The conjecture is then exposed to criticism to find out whether or not that imagined world is anything like the real one. Scientific reasoning is therefore at all levels an interaction between two episodes of thought – a dialogue between two voices, the one imaginative and the other critical; a dialogue, if you like, between the possible and the actual, between proposal and disposal, conjecture and criticism, between what might be true and what is in fact the case.

(Medawar 1972: 22)

So, hypotheses make statements about relations between variables and provide a guide to the researcher as to how the original hunch might be tested. If we hypothesize, because our conjecture suggests it may be so, that age (one variable) has an influence on degree results (another variable), then we can attempt to find out whether that is so – at least, among the subjects in our sample.

In most experimental and some survey studies a hypothesis is postulated, and the research is structured in such a way as to enable the hypothesis to be tested. Some qualitative studies start without a hypothesis or objectives being specified. The investigators will have an idea about what they are doing, but they do not devise detailed procedures before they begin. The study structures the research rather than the other way round (Bogdan and Biklen 1982: 38–44).

There are dangers in this approach, and even experienced researchers occasionally end up with a huge quantity of data and little idea of what to do with it. Collecting everything in sight in the hope that some pattern will emerge is not to be recommended.

Small-scale projects of the kind discussed in this book will not require the statistical testing of hypotheses often required in large-scale sample surveys. Unless your supervisor advises otherwise, a precise statement of objectives is generally quite sufficient. The important point is not so much whether there is a hypothesis, but whether you have carefully thought about what is, and what is not, worth investigating and how the investigation will be conducted. It may be permissible to make minor modifications of objectives as the study proceeds, but that does not obviate the necessity of identifying exactly what you plan to do at the outset. Until that stage has been achieved, it is not possible to consider an appropriate methodology.

The project outline

Before you are ready to submit a project outline to your supervisor, go through all your 'first thoughts' questions again and decide whether any need to be eliminated or refined. Once you are fairly satisfied, decide whether subjects are likely to cooperate and whether you are likely to have the time to collect and analyse the data. This may eliminate questions or amend others. Discussions with colleagues may remind you of important aspects of this study which had not occurred to you. Give yourself a working title and one or two aims – perhaps on the following lines.

Working title: barriers to learning

The final version of the title should tell the reader what the study is about so you will only be ready to devise a final title when you are clear about the focus of the study. 'Barriers to learning' will serve for the time being but, later on, a subtitle will no doubt clarify the nature of the topic.

Aims

1 To investigate whether barriers to learning exist for mature graduates at Bramhope University.
2 If so, to consider what measures might be taken to remove or lessen the impact of such barriers.

Questions to which answers will be needed

1 *Which institutions are to be included in this investigation?*
(Need to ask supervisor's advice about how to go about obtaining permission. Is one institution sufficient? If not, how many?)

2 *What do the institutions mean by 'mature'?*
(21+? 25+? Some other definition? What do *I* mean?)

3 *Is there any relationship between subject/faculty and performance?*
(Find out if institutions have investigated this relationship already. Check source material in the library. No time to read a great deal at this stage, but it would be useful to know if other people have carried out research into this topic. Will require investigation of degree results of mature students in the last 3(?)/5(?) years. Can probably be done, if the institutions agree. Time consuming though. What about performance in first and second year exams and/or course work? That might give a better idea of barriers. Perhaps those who dropped out in the first year would have found some barriers insurmountable. Needs further consideration. Might need some guidance about analysis.)

4 *What barriers to learning do mature students themselves identify?*
(Would need to ask students. Would any definition of 'barriers' be needed, or would that lead students to respond only to what I perceive as being barriers? A questionnaire might be the best way of gathering the basic information, followed by interviews with a sample. Would need to consider how to design, administer and analyse a questionnaire. Perhaps 'normal age' students might be encountering the same barriers, if any. Would that mean I should have to send the same questionnaire to a sample of normal-age students? That would be a big job. Needs thinking about. Would the institutions be willing to release the names and addresses of students? Perhaps not. If not, how would I contact them? There's more to this than meets the eye.)

Systematic examination of questions in this way is an essential stage in the planning process. Do not skimp it. It will save a great deal of time later on and will ensure that what appears in your project outline is likely to be feasible.

Timing

There is never enough time to do all the work that seems to be essential in order to do a thorough job, but if you have a handover date, then somehow the work has to be completed in the specified time. It is unlikely that you will be able to keep rigidly to a timetable, but some attempt should be made to devise a schedule so that you can check progress periodically and, if necessary, force yourself to move from one stage of the research to the next.

If you have to complete more than one project in the year, it is particularly important to produce a list or a chart indicating the stage at which all data should have been collected, analysis carried out and writing begun. Delay on one project means that the timing for the second and third will be upset. It is immaterial whether you produce a list *or* a chart, but some attempt at planning progress should be attempted.

One of the most common reasons for falling behind is that reading takes longer than anticipated. Books and articles have to be located, and the temptation to read just one more book is strong. At some stage a decision has to be made to stop reading, no matter how inadequate the coverage of the subject is. Forcing yourself to move on is a discipline that has to be learnt. Keep in touch with your supervisor about progress.

If things go wrong and you are held up on one stage, there may be other ways of overcoming the problem. Talk about it. Ask for help and advice *before* you become weeks out of phase with your timetable, so that you have a chance of amending your original project plan. The project outline is for guidance only. If subsequent events indicate that it would be better to ask different questions and even to have a different aim, then change while there is time. You have to work to the date specified by the institution, and your supervisor and external examiner will understand that.

Supervision

Somebody told me once about a PhD student who made it clear that he did not need a supervisor and had no intention of attending any research tutorials. He was advised that this would be very unwise and that his chances of succeeding without support were very slight. He persisted and eventually submitted a thesis which proved to be a work of outstanding quality and depth. His external examiner had no doubt in recommending that it was a clear pass. There is a problem with this approach, namely that few people can aspire to such single-mindedness and brilliance. Most of us really do need a supervisor in whom we have confidence, with whom we can share our thinking, who is willing to advise and to give a view about our drafts, and that applies regardless of whether we are working on a 100-hour project, an undergraduate degree or a postgraduate degree.

Student–supervisor relationships

I have occasionally heard students complain that they are getting a raw deal from their supervisors, and in some cases they may have been right – though not always. Supervisors are only human: most will also be lecturing, supervising other students and carry-ing out their own research. Time is generally in short supply and some friends who are heavily committed with supervision have suggested to me that I give the impression that they should be available at all hours to see students on demand who might wish to discuss any aspect of their work, regardless of the time of day, the time involved and the frequency of such requests. Not so. A reasonable balance has to be struck, though I realize that the big question is what 'reasonable' means to both sides.

Phillips and Pugh (1987: 100–16) report a wide variation in student and supervisor expectations and supervisory practice which supported or allegedly impeded students' achievements, as did I in one investigation into barriers to completion of postgrad-uate research degrees (Bell 1996). The majority of the students interviewed had enjoyed very positive relationships with super-visors. Their comments were on the lines of 'very helpful'; 'taught me what research was all about'; 'could not have done this with-out her'; 'he made me believe I could do it, saw me through the bad times, read all my drafts carefully, was straight about what I had written and what more needed to be done'. However, when things went wrong, they went badly wrong, and students' comments were on the lines of 'could never get hold of him'; 'never returned my calls'; 'made me feel inadequate'; 'showed no signs of having read any of my drafts'; 'didn't seem to feel he had any responsibility for advising about my approach'; 'was only willing to see me once a term for a timetabled 20 minutes. He was always late, but always finished on time. I had to travel 100 miles for these 10 minute meetings'; and 'went on study leave, never told me, and no one was allocated to "take me over" at a crucial time in my research when I really needed help'.

Some of the supervisors put up a vigorous defence. Regular telephone calls at 11 p.m. or later in spite of repeated requests not to telephone after 9 p.m. so exasperated one supervisor that he refused to release his home telephone number to his next batch of tutees. There were complaints about students not turning up for arranged meetings; demands for drafts to be read overnight; the assumption that supervisors should always be in their room and available for consultation whenever they were needed, and so on.

The point of raising these issues here is not to lay blame one way or the other but rather to consider ways of avoiding conflict if at all possible, and, only if reason does not prevail, to consider ways of resolving difficult situations.

Codes of practice for supervision

All universities now have (or should have) a code of practice for supervision. However, providing such a code is one thing, and ensuring that everyone involved follows the guidelines may be quite another. You should certainly be able to see your university's or organization's code in order to know what your and your supervisor's rights and responsibilities are. Some universities automatically provide a copy for students; others do not. The code produced by the University of Manchester Institute of Science and Technology (UMIST), which follows what has now become a fairly common format, makes a particular point of saying that

It is important that supervisors and students should, at an early stage, clarify the supervisory arrangements, in order to minimise the risk and problems of misunderstanding, personality clashes, inadequate supervision or unsatisfactory work, the nature of the relationship varying depending on the individuals involved.

(UMIST 1998: paragraph 2 (c))

It is to be hoped that if this advice is followed, potential areas of difficulty can indeed be resolved at an early stage. Even so, supervisor–student relationships do occasionally break down and if all efforts to improve the position fail, then the only thing to do is to request a change before depression and a feeling of hopelessness take over.

Change of supervisor

Achieving a satisfactory change may not always be as easy as it might seem. One part-time student who was not getting on with her supervisor was desperate to change but the department was unable to find another supervisor who was willing to accept her. Having drawn a blank after following all the laid-down procedures, she decided to take action herself. She stood at the door of the postgraduate students' common room one lunch time and shouted 'Is anybody here doing historical research?' When several hands went up, she asked what they thought of their supervisors and what their specialisms were. In desperation, she requested an interview with the supervisor deemed by his students to be 'friendly, helpful, knowledgeable but tough' who eventually, though somewhat reluctantly, agreed to take her on. They got on well and three years later she trod the boards to receive her PhD. Her advice to students in a similar position was:

If you have justifiable concerns, talk about them and try to sort them informally. If that approach fails, go through the formal channels. In my case, neither approach produced the desired changes so I decided I had to take matters into my own hands. I didn't like doing what I did but I would never have completed with the first supervisor. He seemed to leave me feeling that I wasn't intellectually up to research.

Most of the time, everything works well and supervisors are as anxious as their students that they should succeed, but if things go badly wrong, state your case clearly and fairly and don't give in.

Keeping records

Delamont *et al.* (1997: 22) advise supervisors that

> keeping a written record of the supervisory experience signals that you have high expectations of it: that you expect it to last. Keep an agreed record of decisions you have both taken, and make sure you keep a copy in your files. This is particularly valuable if you are ill, or on sabbatical, or away for any reason, and a substitute supervisor has to be involved.

I would add that it is equally important for students to have a copy for their own files. Delamont *et al.* raise what has now become an issue of some importance in these times of increasing litigation: 'It is also invaluable if you end up involved in an appeal or other legal/disciplinary proceedings. It will also help students when they write up the thesis, because key decisions will be "minuted", in your files and in theirs' (p. 22). I couldn't agree more. Unfortunately, disputes have increased and it is as well for both parties to ensure that they have an agreed record of what happened, how many times meetings were arranged, what advice was given and either taken or not taken. Keeping records is not just another attempt at imposing yet another level of useless bureaucracy. It is good professional practice.

The research experience

The supervisor–student relationship at its best will ensure that your research experience will be demanding, but will also be valuable, enjoyable and will result in the successful completion of your investigation – on time. As I have suggested earlier, only isolationist geniuses with plenty of time and a first-class library at their disposal are likely to succeed – and there are not many geniuses around. Most of us need help, encouragement and supervisor expertise. As many first time and experienced researchers have testified, a good supervisor is like gold dust, and by far the most valuable resource we have.

Intellectual property

Last year, I was present at a meeting of postgraduate research students who were discussing their varied research experiences. Discussions started amicably enough but deteriorated when the question of intellectual property was raised. Students wanted a ruling about who had ownership of their research findings and their writing. One complained that his supervisor had encouraged him to submit a paper to a professional journal, based on his research, but then had insisted that his (the supervisor's) name came first. This was considered to be unethical by many of the students, even those who had very good supervision and enjoyed excellent relations with their supervisors.

It is quite customary in scientific and technological departments for supervisors' names to appear on joint papers, the decision about the positioning of the names having been decided by the supervisor and/or in accordance with common departmental or university practice. Where research has been sponsored by government agencies or commercial organizations, universities generally have an agreement in place about intellectual property rights about which students are, or should be, informed at the start of their research. In some cases, students may be required to assign ownership of their intellectual property to the university, to ensure that any potential patent or other rights are not lost, and so it is particularly important that everyone understands what this means.

In education and the social sciences, such precise guidelines are unusual, though universities are now beginning to work through the complex issues of who exactly owns what. Is what students write the property of the university or the organization or research council which funded the research? Is it the property of the researcher alone, or the joint property of the researcher and the supervisor? If it is jointly owned, which name comes first in any published work? The question of the positioning of names may seem trivial, but the importance to organizations, universities and individuals cannot be underestimated. Universities want their research students – and require their academic staff – to publish. Doing well in research assessment exercises brings not only prestige to departments, but also money – and both count. Delamont *et al.* (1997: 22) suggest that

> The supervisor will, depending on the discipline, probably hope that the student will generate publishable findings. It is also useful to decide what will happen about publications by the students (whose name goes first etc.) early on, long before there *are* any publications. However, in science and technology, where joint publication is much more common, the students need to be made aware of the conventions of the discipline, the laboratory and the research group. If the custom of the lab is that *all* publications carry the professor's name, and the supervisor's, the sooner the students understand that, and the reason for it, the better.

They also suggest that supervisors should ensure that students are fully aware of 'the politics of publication, of the research group and the department' (p. 22). But just in case your supervisor ignores this advice or is not aware of its importance, it would be as well to ask to have a copy not only of your university's code of practice for supervisors but also of the agreed policy on intellectual property.

◉ Planning the project checklist

1	Draw up a short list of topics	Consult library catalogues, colleagues and fellow students.
2	Select a topic for investigation.	Discuss possible outcomes with your supervisor and decide what the emphasis of your study is to be.
3	Establish the precise focus of the study.	Draw up a 'first thoughts' list of questions and subject each to rigorous examination.
4	Decide on the aims and objectives of the study or formulate a hypothesis.	Think carefully about what is and what is not worth investigating.
5	Draw up an initial project outline.	List aims and/or objectives, questions to be investigated, possible methods of investigation and literature to be consulted. Consult your supervisor.
6	Read enough to enable you to decide whether you are on the right lines.	The initial reading may give you ideas about approach and methods and how information might be classified.
7	Devise a timetable to enable you to check that all stages will be covered and time allowed for writing.	It is easy to take too long over one stage and so to have insufficient time to carry out essential tasks in the next.
8	Consult your supervisor.	At the stage of deciding on a topic, and after drawing up an initial project outline.
9	Make sure you see your university or college code of practice for supervision.	Do your best to clarify any unclear areas of supervisor/ student rights and responsibilities
10	Keep a brief record of what has been discussed in supervisory tutorials.	It will serve to remind you about what tasks and targets have been agreed.

11 At an appropriate stage in your research, check guidelines on intellectual property.	It is valuable to know who owns what, even though you may have no intention of publishing anything.

Before you begin your preliminary reading, study Chapters 3 and 4.

3

NEGOTIATING ACCESS, ETHICS AND THE PROBLEMS OF 'INSIDE' RESEARCH

No researcher can demand access to an institution, an organization or to materials. People will be doing you a favour if they agree to help, and they will need to know exactly what they will be asked to do, how much time they will be expected to give and what use will be made of the information they provide. Teachers, administrators, parents and keepers of documents will have to be convinced of your integrity and of the value of the research before they decide whether or not to cooperate.

Permission to carry out an investigation must always be sought at an early stage. As soon as you have an agreed project outline and have read enough to convince yourself that the topic is feasible, it is advisable to make a formal, written approach to the individuals and organizations concerned, outlining your plans. Be honest. If you are carrying out an investigation in connection with a diploma or degree course, say that is what you are doing. If you feel the study will probably yield useful and/or interesting information, make a particular point of that – but be careful not to claim more than the investigation merits.

Some institutions and organizations insist that all requests from students wishing to carry out a research project must be agreed by a senior officer and/or, depending on the subject, by an ethics committee. In most cases the head of a school or college will have the authority to grant or to refuse access, but clearing official channels is only the first stage in the process. It is an important stage, but you will also need to be quite sure that the people who actually have to give their time to answer your questions or complete your questionnaires are willing to do so. If you are undertaking an investigation in your own institution and know your colleagues well, you may assume everyone will be willing to help. It is unwise to take their cooperation for granted, particularly if any of them have had a bad experience with other researchers.

Ethical guidelines and protocols

These days, many organizations have gone a long way to formalize research procedures and have produced their own ethical guidelines and protocols. All hospitals and many university departments involved in research with human subjects will have ethics committees which have responsibility for ensuring that any research proposals conform to approved principles and conditions. Without the permission of the ethics committee, research will not be allowed. Certain professional bodies and societies have their own guidelines, which may include issues such as deception concerning the purpose of investigations; encroachment on privacy; confidentiality; safety; care needed when research involves children – and much more. Supervisors should be aware of any restrictions or legal requirements and will ensure that you have appropriate advice about procedures before you begin your data collection; but take care. If you have any doubts about the integrity of your proposal, make sure you consult, discuss your concerns and do not proceed if you or your advisers have any misgivings.

Hart and Bond (1995: 198–201), writing about action research in health and social care, provide examples of different types of codes of practice or protocols which require researchers to ensure that participants are fully aware of the purpose of the research and understand their rights. Some are designed to be read out at the start of interviews, explaining that participation is voluntary, that participants are free to refuse to answer any questions and may withdraw from the interview at any time. Most promise confidentiality and anonymity, but as will be seen later in this chapter, it may be more difficult to fulfil such promises than might at first have been thought. Some suggest that respondents should be asked to sign a copy of the protocol form before the interview begins, indicating that they understand and agree to all the conditions. However, Hart and Bond argue that in their view

> it is not sufficient for the interviewer simply to read it [the protocol] out and then expect the respondent to sign . . . The respondent might justifiably feel anxious about signing anything, particularly at an early stage when the interviewer may be unknown to him or her. In our view it would be better to give the respondent time to read and re-read the protocol for himself or herself at his or her own pace, and to negotiate any additions or changes to it with the researcher. We would also recommend that the respondent should have a signed copy of the form as a record.
>
> (1995: 199)

This is sound advice. In my view, subjects should never be expected to sign any protocol form unless they have had time to read and consider the implications. All researchers will be aiming at the principle of 'informed consent' (see Cohen and Manion 1994: 349–76) which requires careful preparation involving explanation and consultation before any data collecting begins.

Blaxter *et al.* (1996b: 146) summarize the principles of research ethics as follows:

> Research ethics is about being clear about the nature of the agreement you have entered into with your research subjects or contacts. This is why contracts can be a useful device. Ethical research involves getting the informed consent of those you are going to interview, question, observe or take materials from. It involves reaching agreements about the uses of this data, and how its analysis will be reported and disseminated. And it is about keeping to such agreements when they have been reached.

No contract, protocol or code of practice can resolve all problems, but Cohen and Manion (1994: 381) consider that 'a code of ethical practice makes researchers aware of their obligations to their subjects and also to those problem areas where there is a general consensus about what is acceptable and what is not. In this sense it has a clarificatory value'.

Ethical research in practice

The experience of one researcher, Stephen Waters, provides interesting insights into some of the problems that can occur, even in a well-prepared study. He followed the advice of Sapsford and Evans (1984: 270), who suggest that researchers should ask themselves 'Who might be harmed by my research?' And they continue by cautioning that

> Where people are made the subjects of research without their knowledge, and thus have no chance to safeguard their own interests, it should be the special concern of the researcher to look after these interests. The same applies where subjects volunteer for or cooperate with the research but are deceived as to its purpose. The researcher should, ideally, anticipate every possible side-effect of his [*sic*] procedures and guard against them.
>
> (p. 270)

Stephen took note of these warnings and decided to produce his own personal code of practice which made clear the conditions and guarantees within which he felt he must work, in order to ensure his own, his colleagues' and his school's integrity. He had to complete three projects between January and September in connection with an Open University advanced diploma in educational management and decided that, if possible, he would undertake them all in his own school. At the time, he was a teacher of English in a comprehensive school and was interested in investigating the role of his own head of department (called director of English). The director expressed interest in and support for the study, and this convinced Stephen that the topic would be worthwhile and would have a good chance of being successfully completed in the time allowed (effectively three months). The preparation proceeded on the following lines:

1 Informal discussion with the head of the school to obtain agreement in principle.
2 Refinement of the topic, statement of the objectives of the study and preparation of a project outline.
3 Discussion with his tutor and further discussion with the director.
4 Minor adjustments made to the project outline and a consideration of the methods to be used.
5 Formal submission of the project outline to the head, together with names of colleagues he wished to interview and certain guarantees and conditions under which the research would be conducted.

The conditions and guarantees were presented as follows:

1 All participants will be offered the opportunity to remain anonymous.
2 All information will be treated with the strictest confidentiality.
3 Interviewees will have the opportunity to verify statements when the research is in draft form.
4 Participants will receive a copy of the final report.
5 The research is to be assessed by the Open University for examination purposes only, but should the question of publication arise at a later date, permission will be sought from the participants.
6 The research will attempt to explore educational management in practice. It is hoped the final report may be of benefit to the school and to those who take part.

So how did it go? This is what Stephen wrote after the project was completed.

> I felt that presenting the guarantees formally was essential. As I was completely inexperienced in research, I had to assure the headmaster that the fieldwork would be carried out with integrity and convince him that he could place his trust in

me. Simon's warning was still fresh in my mind, that 'however harmonious relationships in a school appear to be, however democratic the organization, trust does not automatically exist between professionals. It has to be created' (Simons 1984: 127). Moreover, I wished to convince all participants that there was to be, in the words of Preedy and Riches (1985: 4) 'some payoff for them in giving access'.

With hindsight, I should have exercised greater caution. Condition 3 could not be met in full since I later found that, although a proper check could be made to verify statements participants had made while being interviewed, there was insufficient time for them to proofread a full draft. Condition 4 was fulfilled but the cost proved to be prohibitive and I decided to eliminate this condition when the other two case studies were undertaken. This experience certainly alerted me to the danger of promising too much too soon.

It was only when the time drew near for the findings of my research to be disseminated that I became aware of the two areas where the wording of my conditions of research was open to interpretation. The first was that, in promising confidentiality (Condition 2), I had not made it clear what the implications of releasing information would be. As there was insufficient time to release a draft report, no one could check whether my interpretation of what they had said was fair. In any case, as the headmaster was the only person to hold a written copy of my guarantees, the respondents could only interpret the conditions under which they had agreed to participate from my verbal explanation. In retrospect, it would have been better to have provided a duplicated explanation of the course and a written outline of my intentions. Teachers are busy people and it was unreasonable to assume that they would be able to remember a conversation which had taken place some time before their services were formally required. As it was, whether or not they remembered the guarantees, they were totally dependent on my integrity to present their views in a balanced, objective manner.

More naïvely, until I was writing the first report, I had not realized that identifying people by role may preserve the guarantee of anonymity for an outside reader, but it did not confer the same degree of obscurity for those within the school. Fortunately, my failure to clarify these matters did not lead to problems – but it could have done.

Stephen Waters learnt a great deal from his first experience of conducting an investigation. He felt he had made some mistakes at his first attempt and was uneasy because he had not been able to fulfil all the conditions and guarantees. He had prepared the ground very well but had not fully appreciated the time and effort involved in reporting back to colleagues and in producing copies of reports. He was concerned at his lack of precision in defining exactly what he meant by anonymity and confidentiality, and made quite sure that in subsequent investigations he clarified the position. He found it harder to know what to do about role conflict. He was a full-time teacher and a part-time researcher – a not unusual combination – and on occasion found it difficult to reconcile the two roles. There were definite advantages in being an 'inside' researcher. For example, he had an intimate knowledge of the context of the research and of the micropolitics of the institution, travel was not a problem and subjects were easily reached. He knew how best to approach individuals and appreciated some of their difficulties. He found that colleagues welcomed the opportunity to air problems and to have their situation analysed by someone who understood the practical day-to-day realities of their task. On the other hand, he found interviewing some colleagues an uncomfortable experience for both parties. As an insider, he quickly came to realize that you have to live with your mistakes after completing the research. The close contact with the institution and colleagues made objectivity difficult to attain and, he felt, gaining confidential knowledge had the potential for affecting his relationship with colleagues. In the event, this did not seem to be the case, but he could foresee situations where problems might have arisen.

When he had successfully completed the diploma course, he was asked whether he felt it had all been worthwhile and whether he had any comments that might be helpful to others who were undertaking a research project for the first time. He wrote as follows:

I may have given the impression that my research was so fraught with difficulties that it was counter-productive. If so, it is because I wish to encourage the prospective inside-researcher to exercise caution and to be aware of possible pitfalls. In reality, I enjoyed my research immensely and found that the experience of interviewing a cross-section of teaching staff provided me with a much greater working knowledge of the school's management practices. Indeed, my research was so absorbing that at times I found myself struggling to keep pace with my teaching commitments. From Peeke's description, it appears that this problem is not uncommon among teacher-researchers. 'To be a successful researcher can demand a lessening commitment to the task of teacher; it is ironic that a concern for the quality of education may motivate a teacher to involve himself/herself in research, but can also be detrimental to a teacher's own work in the classroom' (Peeke 1984: 24).

I am certain, even without hindsight, that I could have done little to resolve this dilemma. I can honestly say that my research has made me more understanding of the problems confronting those responsible for running the school and has subsequently provoked a great deal of thought about educational issues. If my research had not been practically relevant I would have felt concerned about the extent of my commitment to it. As it was, several recommendations which appeared in my first report have been taken up by the school; my third report on the role of the governing body in the curriculum was placed on the agenda of a governors' meeting in spring and many colleagues have been complimentary about the content of the case studies in general. If I had to choose one strategy that I would encourage prospective inside researchers to adopt, it would be to relate the research report to the pragmatic concerns of the institution. Perhaps, as Vyas (1979) suggests, that is how to overcome the dichotomy between research and practice and the way in which to persuade one's colleagues that participation in research will be as beneficial to them as it is to the researcher.

Whether or not you relate your research to the pragmatic concerns of the institution depends on the nature of your task and your own special concerns, but whether you are an inside or outside researcher, whether you are full-time or part-time, experienced or inexperienced, care has to be taken to consult, to establish guidelines and to make no promises that cannot be fulfilled. Common sense and courtesy will go a long way to establishing good practice, but remember that research generally takes longer than you think it will, so when you begin the process of negotiating access and checking any ethical guidelines or protocols, look through the following checklist to make sure you have remembered everything and to try to ensure you do not take on more than you can manage.

⊙ **Negotiating access, ethics and the problems of 'inside' research checklist**

1 Clear official channels by formally requesting permission to carry out your investigation as soon as you have an agreed project outline.

Check regulations regarding ethical guidelines and protocols.

2 Speak to the people who will be asked to cooperate.

Getting the management's permission is one thing, but you need to have the support of the people who will be asked to give interviews or complete questionnaires.

3 Maintain strict ethical standards at all times.

Consult your supervisor if you become concerned about the way the research is developing.

4 Submit the project outline to the head/principal, senior officer, or ethics committee, if necessary.

List people you would like to interview or to whom you wish to send questionnaires and state conditions under which the study will be conducted.

5 Decide what you mean by anonymity and confidentiality.

Remember that if you are writing about 'the head of English' and there is only one head of English, the person concerned is immediately recognizable.

6 Decide whether participants will receive a copy of the report and/or see drafts or interview transcripts.

There are cost and time implications. Think carefully before you make promises.

7 Inform participants what is to be done with the information they provide.

Your eyes and those of the examiner only?

8 Prepare an outline of intentions and conditions under which the study will be carried out to hand to participants.

Even if you explain the purpose of the study and the conditions/guarantees verbally, participants may forget.

9 Be honest about the purpose of the study and about the conditions of the research.

If you say an interview will last ten minutes, you will break faith if it lasts an hour. If you are conducting the investigations as part of a degree or diploma course, say so.

10 Remember that people who agree to help are doing you a favour.

Make sure you return papers and books in good order and on time. Letters of thanks should be sent, no matter how busy you are.

11 Never assume 'it will be all right'. Negotiating access is an important stage in your investigations.

If you are an inside-researcher, you will have to live with your mistakes, so take care.

12 If you have doubts about the ethics of your research, consult your supervisor and decide what action to take.

A *word of warning*. If at some time in the future, colleagues or other research workers ask you for cooperation with a project, would you be willing to give the same amount of time and effort as you are asking for yourself? If not, perhaps you are asking too much.

Further reading

Berger, R.M. and Patchner, M.A. (1994) 'Research ethics' in Bennett, N., Glatter, R. and Levačić, R. *Improving Educational Management through Research and Consultancy*, pp. 93–8. London: Paul Chapman.

Blaxter, L., Hughes, C. and Tight, M. *et al.* (1996) *How to Research*. Buckingham: Open University Press. Pages 145–9 deal with ethical issues.

Cohen, L. and Manion, L. (1994) 'The ethics of educational and social research', Chapter 16, pp. 347–84 in *Research Methods in Education*. London: Routledge.

Hart, E. and Bond, M. (1995) *Action Research for Health and Social Care: A Guide to Practitioners*. Buckingham: Open University Press. Pages 198–201 provide examples of ethics protocols.

May, T. (1993) *Social Research: Issues, Methods and Process*. Buckingham: Open University Press. Pages 41–8 consider ethical issues in social research.

4

KEEPING RECORDS, MAKING NOTES AND LOCATING LIBRARIES

Before you continue with your planning, it is important to check that as a researcher you are familiar with methods of keeping records and making notes. It is very common for experienced professionals to dismiss the notion that they require any reminders about how to keep records or to make notes. However, experience has shown that no matter how sophisticated we are as learners and researchers, we all need to be reminded about the importance of systematic recording. The skills involved are all part of the researcher's tools of the trade.

Finding information in the first place can be hard enough. Finding it again some time afterwards can be even harder unless your methods of recording and filing are thorough and systematic. We all think we shall remember, but, after several weeks of reading, analysing and selecting, memory becomes faulty. After a few months, we may vaguely recall having read something some time about the topic being studied, but when and where escapes us. After a longer period, the chances of remembering are remote. So everything that is read must be noted, and the sooner some systematic system of record-keeping is started, the better.

It may seem a waste of time to record a source which proves to be of no use or interest, but there must have been some reason why you decided to look at it in the first place. The title may have sounded interesting, or you may have read other works by the same author that impressed you. It would follow then that some time ahead, the title may still sound interesting and the author may still be remembered as having produced quality work in another context. You may come across the reference again, and ask to borrow the book again. All this is a waste of time, and in any investigation, whether small or large scale, there is never enough time to do everything that has to be done. A note to remind you why you decided the work was of no interest would be enough to jog your memory and to enable you to abandon that particular line of inquiry.

The card index

In the early days of an investigation it may seem enough to jot down a reference on the back of an envelope, but old envelopes thrown into a box will not provide you with a reliable resource, and the likelihood is that references will be incomplete and difficult to track down at a later stage. If you are only going to need half a dozen references, then scraps of paper may serve, but as your investigation proceeds, you will accumulate many sources of information, and an orderly system is necessary from the beginning. Most research workers will acknowledge that they have wasted valuable time tracing books, periodicals or quotations because they forgot to note the reference at the time, or because they inexplicably left off the name of the journal, the author or the date.

I still use cards. I don't own a laptop computer and in any case, portable they may be but they are still heavy to carry around. Cards weigh practically nothing, cost practically nothing, fit comfortably into a shoe box and as long as you always have a few in your pocket, you will always be in a position to make a full record of sources on the spot, wherever the spot might be. I keep copies for everything. I'm a 'what if-er'. What if I lose all my cards? What if I accidentally throw them away? What if . . .? So, I transfer card information onto my computer as soon as I can. That provides the second copy *and* gives me the beginnings of a full list of references, in alphabetical order. I am even more of a what if-er as far as the computer is concerned. What if a power cut loses all my work or, more probably, what if I press the wrong button one day and send ten chapters into oblivion? Backup disks of course, and that gives me my third record – just to be sure. It really is immaterial which method you select to make copies as long as copies are made. Some colleagues consider my obsession for keeping copies in various forms is excessive. Perhaps they are right, but we all have our own way of working and don't let anyone tell you there is only one way of doing things.

Computers have transformed life for us all. I go back to the days when hardly anyone had a computer and producing a book, report or thesis meant typing and retyping. If a paragraph happened to be in the wrong position, well tough. Type that page again. Now, we can cut, copy, paste and clear in seconds. It used to be a major job drawing graphs, diagrams and charts and I at least could never manage to make a decent job of it. Now, incompetent though I am computationally, even I can make a fair shot at instructing the computer how to do the job for me.

But I still use 6 × 4 inch (15 × 10 centimetre) cards, which generally have enough space for additional items such as the international standard book number (ISBN) which allows librarians and booksellers to locate titles; perhaps a note to indicate which library holds the book or journal; reference to particular chapters or pages relating to special topics – or anything else which might be useful. The cards will be your portable stock-in-trade and you should start building up your stock as soon as you begin your research.

Referencing

There are several perfectly acceptable ways of recording sources and other information, and most educational institutions will have a preferred 'house' style which you will be expected to adopt.

If you are left to decide yourself, you will need to consider which of the available options suits you best.

Different publishers adopt different styles. Look at the Bibliographies or References at the end of several books. The likelihood is that you will find different approaches, though each will contain the following information:

For books

Author's surname and forename or initials
Date of publication
Title (underlined in typescript: italics in print)
Place of publication
Name of publisher

For articles and chapters in books

Author's surname and forename or initials
Date of publication
Title (in inverted commas)
Source of the article or chapter, namely:
      Title of the journal or book (underlined or in italics)
      Volume number, issue and page numbers in journals

The Harvard method, which I use in this book, has a number of advantages over other methods. It avoids footnotes, which are awkward to deal with. All sources mentioned in the text appear at the end of the book or report and not chapter by chapter. When sources are referred to in the text, names of authors and date of publication only will appear. For example 'As Delamont *et al.* (1997: 47) say . . .' The full details of the book will then appear in the alphabetic list of references at the end of the report, thesis or book, and all names included in the '*et al.*' will be given, on the following lines:

Delamont, S., Atkinson, P. and Parry, O. (1997) *Supervising the PhD: A Guide to Success*. Buckingham, The Society for Research into Higher Education and Open University Press.

Et al. is used when there are three or more authors, but where there are only two, both names are included.

If Delamont, Atkinson and Parry had more than one publication in 1997, then suffixes 'a' and 'b' would be added. For example, in the text there would be Delamont *et al.* (1997a) or (1997b) and their names would again be given in full, together with the 'a' or 'b' in the list of references and on your card. If several of their books are cited which were published in different years, then these would be listed in chronological order.

You might wish to add certain information or memory joggers to the card. If so, it might look something like the following:

Delamont, S., Atkinson, P. and Parry, O. (1997) *Supervising the PhD: A Guide to Success.* Buckingham, The Society for Research into Higher Education and Open University Press.

ISBN no. 0 335 19516 4 (pbk)

See page 47 re ethics.

A word about the way this card has been displayed. There is no reason why a full stop should appear after the title. You could use a comma or leave a space. Nor is there any reason why the second line should be indented. If you wanted to, you could put the authors' names in capitals, as in some of the following examples. However, bear in mind that universities and publishers will have their own guidelines and it is as well to conform to their preferred style. If there are no guidelines, and if you decide another format looks better, then adopt that, but remember, once you have decided on a system, you should stick to it.

Records of articles in journals or articles in collections have certain differences, as illustrated opposite.

Articles in journals

> GLATTER, R. (1997) 'Context and Capability in Educational Management', *Educational Management and Administration*, 25(2), pp. 181–192.

Articles in collections

> BAKER, S. and CARTY, J. (1994) 'Literature Searching, Finding, Organizing and Recording Information' in Bennett, N., Glatter, R. and Levačić, R. (eds) *Improving Educational Management through Research and Consultancy*, London, Paul Chapman in association with the Open University.

Referencing can take up an irritatingly long time if you have to keep checking back, so good habits established early in your investigations will pay off later on. If your cards and computer records are in good order, drawing up your final list of references will only be a matter of transferring the information from card to computer to paper or selecting sources cited in your text from your computer list. However, it is at this stage that consistent recording will pay off. It is not permissible to use the Harvard system for one reference, the British system for another and a method of your own for a third.

It takes a little time to remember all the detail of what must be underlined (or in italics) and what appears in inverted commas; where dates appear, how to deal with quotations and the type of punctuation you selected. Once you have mastered the detail, it becomes automatic to record *all* sources as soon as you come across them, *in the same consistent format.* Until you are absolutely confident about what goes where, you might wish to keep model cards in your card index just to check that all the essential information has been recorded.

Note-taking and preparation for the report

In addition to recording bibliographical details, you will need to devise a system of note-taking which records the actual evidence obtained from your sources. Some researchers prefer notebooks, some prefer loose sheets of paper, some carry a laptop computer or palmtop around with them, and others prefer cards. If you use a notebook, information will be recorded as it is obtained. Leave a wide margin and only write on one side of the paper. At a later stage you may wish to cut up the notebook, preferably into pieces of uniform size, to enable you to sort material into sections ready for trying out a structure (the analytical framework) for your final report. Whether you use notebooks, loose sheets, laptops or cards will depend on your preference, but the type of information you record and the method of recording will always be the same.

At one stage in my life, I decided that my home was not big enough to contain any more files of notes, so I developed the practice of cutting up paper to the size of my index cards. Now, I staple notes to the cards. Yards of them sometimes. When I told one very computer-competent student of my method he looked at me in disbelief and said 'Oh really!' Well, as I always seem to be saying, what suits one doesn't suit another. Decide what your own preferred approach is and try not to listen to anyone who says to you 'Oh really!' in a disapproving voice.

Orna (1995: 48) strongly recommends that we should organize a method of indexing our notes. That is obviously sound advice, although she acknowledges that producing an index which provides easy access to whatever we need to know is not easy:

> . . . by the very fact of bringing items together in *one* way (by author, by main subject, by date of addition to the store,

for example), it separates items that have *other* things in common. The same author may have written articles on a number of quite different subjects, so while that arrangement makes it easy to find everything by a given author, it makes it hard to find items on a given subject.

(Orna 1995: 49)

Well, life was never meant to be easy and we just have to do the best we can to ensure we have some sort of indexing and reference system which is easy to maintain and which is likely to give us reasonable access to most of the source material and topics in our store. As Orna says, 'there is no "right way" of doing it and successful researchers use a wide variety of strategies' (p. 36).

The categorization of evidence

All your preliminary work is leading up to the writing of your report, dissertation or thesis. If you have already identified chapter headings, you have the beginnings of a map which will develop as you go along. It will almost certainly include some topics, key words or categories which you think might well prove to be of significance. If the categories elude you at the start of your research, they will emerge as you read. Your first choice of categories (your hunches) may in any case prove to be unsuitable; adjustments may be needed and additions made as your understanding of the subject grows.

One of the easiest ways of producing a rough-and-ready index system is to make a note on your bibliographic cards of likely or potential key words as they emerge from your reading. I used to write them in colour or else highlight them at the top of the card. Students set me right on that and said it was more sensible to write them in pencil, so they could be eliminated or recategorized later, if necessary. Well, I'm always willing to learn and so I adopt that system now. However, if you have boxes full of bibliographic cards and are trying to locate sources relating to one topic, it will be time-consuming to make your way through them all. As likely categories emerge, you may wish to open category cards. So in your research into barriers to learning experienced by mature students, you might have cards relating to performance in examinations; age; previous educational experience; family commitments; availability of books; level of financial support, etc. A category card headed 'age v. degree performance' would contain all sources relating to that important topic on the lines of author, date and page. When you come to produce your drafts, your groupings will be ready and all you have to do is refer back to your original notes (which in my case will always be attached to the bibliographic card) to check on matters of detail.

Noting quotations

A particularly perceptive observation by an author may often illustrate a point you wish to make in an assignment or report, and add an extra dimension to your argument. Making a note of quotations at the time you read them is as important as recording the full bibliographical information about the source. When you are writing up your final report, you will not have time to recall books from the library, nor to search in the used envelope box. If a particular sentence or paragraph strikes you at the time of reading as being a potential quotation, note it carefully, record the chapter and page number, show clearly if you have left out any word or words by adding three full stops, and file it where you know you will be able to find it, even if this requires some cross-referencing in your card index. If you have the facilities, it is an even better idea to photocopy the extract, adding details about source in the usual way, and attaching it to your card. (Library staff will advise about copyright regulations.) If you are unable to photocopy, then make it quite clear which is the quotation and which is your paraphrase, or when you come to write up your project you may find you are committing the sin of using someone else's words as your own.

A lot of fuss about nothing?

Well no. Just acquiring the tools of the trade. Referencing can be irritatingly pernickety, but once you have established a routine, recording information becomes automatic and no problem at all. If you assimilate the information in this chapter and if you record your sources accurately and consistently, you will have begun to establish good research habits and to lay the foundations of your own research. You will be rewarded for your hard work if not in heaven, then certainly when you come to write your report. You will be able to locate information easily, to regroup and reclassify evidence and to produce quotations to support your arguments. However, before you can do any of these things, you will need to ensure you have access to a good library – and in these days of reduced budgets and charges for services, that may not be as automatic as it once was.

Access to libraries

As far as I am concerned, researchers cannot manage without libraries and the service of librarians. As Sally Baker makes clear in the next chapter, you may be able to access certain computer databases from your own home, if you have the equipment, the expertise and have negotiated access to specialist network resources. However, even if you follow this route, you will still need to have library access in order to consult books and, even more particularly, journals.

If you work in or are registered as a student in a university or college, you should normally have full access to their libraries and to many or all of the services they provide. If no mention is made of what library and computer facilities are available when you apply for any course, make sure you ask *before you register*. You *will need* these services.

We all think we know how to use libraries, and certainly it would not take any of us long to get to grips with the system operating and the stock held by small branch libraries. Finding our way round and discovering what stock is held in main public and specialist libraries in universities and large colleges is quite another matter. They can seem like Aladdin's caves for students and researchers. They hold treasures that dazzle; but caves can be dangerous. It is easy to get lost and to become so anxious not to leave any of the treasures behind that it becomes impossible ever to leave. All this is rather fanciful, but many a research project has foundered because of undisciplined reading and failure to make full use of all the facilities libraries offer.

There have been massive changes in the way libraries organize their print material and in the development of computer databases which (in subscribing institutions) give us access to on-line datasets which can provide invaluable information relating to citation indexes, bibliographic details of journal articles, book reviews and access to many worldwide networks. The Aladdin's cave has become very fancy indeed and it can take some time to get to grips with the many and varied computer-generated systems now available in large libraries, which can provide us with such riches – but only if we know how to use them.

One problem facing researchers is that librarians have different views about how their stock should be organized and which online systems should be subscribed to. It takes time to familiarize ourselves with the layout of the libraries we are using and to find out, for example:

• where the current and back issues of periodicals are shelved, whether they are in hard copy, or in microform, and which titles, if any, are available only electronically;
• if there are special reserve or short-term loan collections of books, and whether all the book stock is held on site;
• which bibliographies, indexes and abstracts are in stock, and in which formats; if there are any specialist bibliographies for your subject area; whether the reference section – encyclopaedias, directories, dictionaries, yearbooks – is separated into quick, general or subject reference collections.

Many libraries provide printed guides, which can help you to find your way around fairly quickly. There is generally plenty of help and advice to be found on the library web pages (though you will for sure need to learn how to use that facility). However, the key to a library's holding is the catalogue. Most library catalogues are now on-line and are often referred to as OPACs (on-line public access catalogues). Not only can you find out what is held in stock by the library you are using, you can also search the catalogues of other libraries by using an OPAC. On-screen menus guide you to search by author, title or subject, and you can find out which libraries hold the material that will be of most use for your research. Magic – but there may just be a few problems. For example, you may not be entitled to use all libraries (though a courteous enquiry may sometimes produce a helpful response). However, all these doors will be closed to you unless you are able to find a library within reasonable travelling distance of your home base which will at least grant you reference, but far more importantly, lending rights.

Academic libraries

The libraries of academic institutions will probably hold most of the specialized resources you will need for your research, but unless you are a member of staff or a student of the institution, you will have to find out exactly what services you are permitted to use. Some libraries will not allow you any access at all; others will allow you reference access to their collections, but this means you will only be able to consult books, journals, bibliographies, reference works and so on. Some will allow you to use only print materials (hard copy) and, because of the terms of various licences, will not be able to give you any access to on-line resources other than OPACs. Some libraries charge even for reference access to their collections; others will allow you to become an external borrower for a fee, occasionally with the option of using the interlibrary loan service. They may have specific restrictions on the number of books you may borrow and the range of collections from which you can select books. Make sure you check that you will be allowed to use the material you need *before you make any payment.*

If it is possible for you to use the World Wide Web, you can find out academic libraries' conditions of use throughout the country by checking the individual library websites via the University of Wolverhampton UK Sensitive Map, located at: http://www.scit. wlv.ac.uk/ukinfo/uk.map.html. This website also provides a route to the OPACs of individual libraries in higher education in the UK, and you can save yourself wasted journeys by checking the catalogue on-line. In addition, once you have reached the libraries' web pages, you will also be able to find other useful general information such as opening hours in term time and during vacations.

Public libraries

Fortunately, although available services vary, the access restrictions mentioned above do not apply to the use of public libraries. Some of the larger city public libraries hold excellent reference collections. The overall collection has to be general in scope, but you can often find a selection of important education and social science journals, as well as some of the abstracts and indexes you will need to find out what books and articles have been published in these subject areas. By using these, and following up with requests to the interlibrary loan service (there is a charge for this service) to obtain those items which are not held by the library, you should have access to much of the published literature. As the interlibrary loan process can often be quite lengthy, you will have more chance of obtaining material within your deadline if you make your request as soon as you possibly can.

Many public libraries now give access to the Internet though once again there is a charge for this, and charges can mount up over the period of a research project. However, even if you are unable to obtain access to a university or college library, public libraries should be able to fulfil most of your information needs if you allow enough time. If you need help on how to make the best of what is available, *remember to ask the library staff*. They know what stock and what Internet and other facilities they have and sometimes, for example, bibliographies that are used by librarians are not on open access, though you should normally be able to consult them on request.

Finally, you can access the websites of UK and European libraries for additional information on-line at this website address: http://dspace.dial.pipex.com/town/square/ac940/ukpublib.html.

An abundance of riches but . . .

The services and systems which are now available to researchers are amazingly good and if you are working on a PhD, for example, you should do your best to become familiar with what is on offer. However, if you are working on a 100-hour project, a reasonable local library and the resources of your own school, college or other place of employment may well provide you with sufficient materials to enable you to get an idea of what work has already been done in your own or similar subject areas. The amount of background information you will need will depend entirely on the size, depth and context of your research topic and you may not need to use any of the computer-generated databases though they can save a great deal of time. There are dangers though: it is very easy to be seduced by the vast amount of information they produce unless you are very precise about what it is you need to know.

Contrary to popular opinion, not all researchers own, have the use of or want anything to do with computers and they can still manage to produce good quality research. However, computers are a useful aid, like vacuum cleaners and washing machines. Once we learn how to use them, they can save us hours and weeks of hard labour, but the key to success is learning how to make the best use of what they have to offer. That can take some time, but it will generally be time well spent.

In the next chapter, Sally Baker takes us through the complexities of literature searching and provides us with information about what we might expect to find via the Internet and in academic and large public libraries. You may not need all the information she provides at first, but you will most certainly need to be aware of the procedures involved in locating sources before you begin your own search. It might be helpful to read the first part of the chapter which relates directly to the procedures involved in literature searching (search techniques, search structure, selecting keywords, managing information, citations and references, and evaluating sources) and the final sections describing how one search of literature relating to mature student drop-out was carried out. You might then decide to skim through the paragraphs on sources of information until you are ready to begin your own search (bibliographies, finding journal articles, finding official publications, theses, Internet resources, search engines, and Internet gateways) and to use those sections for reference purposes. Before you begin your own search, you might find it a useful training exercise to follow the same mature student drop-out pathways as Sally – just to make sure you are completely familiar and comfortable with the procedures involved.

⊙ **Keeping records, making notes and locating libraries checklist**

1 Make a note of everything you read.	Even note the items that were no use.
2 Start a card index as soon as you begin your investigations.	Select a card size and stick to it.
3 When recording sources, make sure you always note author's name and initials, date of publication, title (underlined in typescript, in inverted commas for articles), place of publication and publisher.	There are variations for books, articles in collections and journal articles. Make out model cards as memory joggers.
4 Decide on a system of referencing and stick to it.	The Harvard system is the easiest to manage.
5 Decide whether to use a notebook, loose sheets, computers or cards for note-taking.	Use one side of paper or cards to ease sorting, and devise an index system.
6 Devise a 'first thoughts' list of categories.	Devise a subject key, if necessary. Write the categories and/or key words in pencil in case changes are needed later on.
7 Make an accurate note of all quotations.	Note any omissions by (. . .); make clear what is a direct quotation and what is your paraphrase. Photocopy extracts if possible, then you know there are no errors.
8 Whatever method and format you adopt, BE CONSISTENT.	
9 Negotiate access to a library as soon as you possibly can.	You cannot demand the right to use the facilities of academic and specialist libraries, and even if permission is given, there may sometimes be a charge.

10 Take time to become familiar with your library print materials and on-line facilities.

But make sure you do not become seduced by the amount of material the on-line systems produce.

11 REMEMBER that it is still possible to produce good research without access to computer databases.

But the riches to be found from databases can be worth the effort of finding out how to to exploit them.

5

FINDING AND SEARCHING INFORMATION SOURCES

Sally Baker

You have drawn up your shortlist of topics, focused your study, and now you need to find out what has been published in your subject area. This chapter does not aim to provide an exhaustive list of information sources, but is intended to help you to find a route through the range of materials available to you, to help you to plan and carry out a literature search.

The main *secondary sources* will be identified. These are the bibliographies, indexes and abstracts that you can use to help you to find the *primary sources* – the full text of articles, books, government reports, etc. that you need to read for your research project.

In the last few years the increase in the amount of information that can be found on-line has been enormous. Many bibliographic sources are available in several formats – as hard copy, on CD-ROM, and on-line via the Internet. If you have on-line access via a computer it is possible to search for the details of books, journal articles and conference proceedings, as well as for data such as statistics, maps, contacts in organizations, e-mail addresses and so on. You may also be able to access on-line the full text of many of the primary sources you need, particularly journal articles. The number of periodical titles that are available electronically is growing rapidly.

However, although it is normally quicker to search in this way, it can be expensive. Most information is available from several different sources (indeed, no source is comprehensive) and you need not feel that you have to have access to all those listed here. For this reason, on-line and printed resources are included to give you a choice about how you search for information – both tabletop and laptop – according to your individual circumstances.

'Tabletop' is used in the sense of visiting a library, searching through printed indexes and abstracts, physically handling bibliographic sources and noting down the details. 'Laptop' refers to looking at resources on-line, perhaps from a computer at home, at work or in a library, searching for information electronically and printing out the results. As your literature search progresses, however, you will probably use a combination of these approaches.

Literature searching

If you have been given a topic for investigation, then you will no doubt have been provided with a list of books, articles or other material that is required or recommended reading for your subject area. For a small project you may not need to go beyond this reading list. If you are choosing your own research area or have still to decide on the precise focus of your investigation, then you will need to find out what has been published in your field. Search techniques are the same for both a small- or a large-scale project. The difference lies in the amount of time you spend on a literature search and the number of sources you use: the more advanced the research, the more extensive your search will need to be.

It is important to plan your search or searches – with a lengthy research project you will probably carry out several to update yourself on additions to the literature – and to keep your aim in view. Try to avoid feeling that you have to attempt to find everything ever written in your area. It can be dispiriting to find yourself bogged down by a mass of information, with little time left to actually read what you have found.

Planning your literature search: search techniques

The aim of your search is to retrieve information of direct relevance to your research and to avoid being sidetracked or overloaded with material of only peripheral interest. This seems obvious, but searching effectively means that you must be systematic not only about how and where you search, but also about recording the details of what you find as you go along. It is equally important to think critically about what you actually select to read from all the references you retrieve.

Although you will not be able to decide finally until you see the references resulting from your search, you should consider at an early stage some search parameters. For example:

- How far back will you look for material? The last five/ten years?
- Do you plan only to read material published in the UK? The USA? Australia?
- What type of material do you want to trace? Books, journals, theses, government reports, Internet resources?
- Do you want material only in English, or in other languages?

In most cases you will have a finite period in which to complete your project. If you are not to waste valuable time, it is important to try to define precisely what you are looking for as soon as you can. Often, however, you can get a clearer focus as you prepare your search and begin your initial trawl of the literature, simply by being able to identify what you are *not* looking for.

Search structure

The Figure 5.1 illustrates the basic structure of a subject search. You may be researching the academic performance of mature students in higher education. If you break your topic down into its component subject parts – 'mature students', 'academic performance' and 'higher education' – and represent each component by a circle as the diagram shows, the information you are aiming for, which will contain all three elements of your topic, occurs at the shaded intersection of the circles.

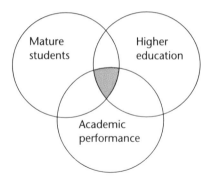

Figure 5.1 Literature search model.

This is the kind of figure that it is useful to bear in mind if you are carrying out an on-line search – your laptop approach. You can enter as many subject keywords as you think are relevant for each component of your topic. The computer will automatically combine the subject terms for you when you perform the search.

However, if you are carrying out the tabletop search, then arriving at this information intersection depends on you. Printed sources have to be searched using individual terms. To use the example above ('academic performance of mature students in higher education') you may, during the course of your search, come across a subject term 'lifelong learners' that you have not searched under before. You may well think it worthwhile to go through all the sources you have already searched using this new term. To do this each time you find an additional subject heading is time-consuming, and you have to have been meticulous about noting those sources and which keywords you have already searched to avoid further duplication of effort. A tabletop search via printed sources is linear in its execution, but you have the opportunity to browse, to see adjacent subject terms, and perhaps to discover something relevant by chance. Serendipity is rarer in a computer search because it is more difficult to browse.

References from printed bibliographies have to be written down by hand or photocopied, whereas references found on-line can be downloaded, printed out or e-mailed. The 'tabletopper' is at considerable advantage over the 'laptopper', however, on those occasions when the printer will not work, the computer system freezes up and will not give you access to those references you have carefully marked, or the network goes down and you cannot access the references you have e-mailed to yourself.

Selecting keywords

To avoid making the focus of your search too narrow, and restricting the number of references you retrieve, you should organize your topic into subject groups or *sets*, and analyse the keywords in each to try to find as many relevant search terms as possible. You might use a thesaurus (e.g. the *British Education Thesaurus*) which lists synonyms and related words, to help you to think of broader and narrower terms and alternative spellings. Some computer databases have an on-line subject thesaurus which you can use to find additional terms during your search.

Taking the topic illustrated by Figure 5.1 as an example, your list might expand considerably. If you use 'AND' with 'OR' (known as 'Boolean operators') you can see how the sets can be combined logically to retrieve the references that contain all three elements as illustrated by Figure 5.1:

- Set 1: mature students OR adult education OR adult learning OR adult students OR continuing education OR non-traditional students OR lifelong learning **AND**
- Set 2: academic performance OR academic achievement OR academic ability OR learner outcomes **AND**
- Set 3: higher education OR colleges OR universities OR post-secondary education.

As you search, you will probably amend your list to include additional keywords or you may jettison broader terms that retrieve large numbers of references too general to be of use. It may be only at this point that you can define what you *don't* want. The inclusion of 'lifelong learning' and 'post-secondary education' among your search terms, for example, may give you too many references to non-graduate qualifications or to the further education sector to be of relevance to a research topic that focuses on university degrees.

It can be helpful when you find a relevant reference to note down any subject headings, sometimes called 'identifiers' or 'descriptors' that have been used to index it. The need to modify your list of keywords as you search means that you must remember to note where and what you have searched, and what you have found.

Managing information

Even if you decide to dispense with spending any time on the planning stage of your search, *do take note of this section*. Researchers with unlimited time may decide to plunge straight into a literature search without preparation and hope for the best. However, just as you become a more efficient researcher by adopting a systematic approach to planning and conducting literature searches, so, too, your research will benefit if you manage information effectively. Unfortunately, from the number of whey-faced academics and researchers about to submit papers or theses who are found panicking in libraries as they desperately search for missing sources, page numbers, authors' initials and so on, it is apparent that even an occasional lapse in recording bibliographic details can result in hours of wasted time at the point when time is particularly short. It is inevitable that you will from time to time lack a similar detail from a reference – sometimes as a result of others' incorrect referencing – but if you adopt a disciplined approach to information management you will be able to minimize the number of occasions when this occurs.

Citations and references

In Chapter 4 you were given detailed advice on recording sources of information and examples of how to construct references for different types of material. As has already been emphasized you must acknowledge your sources to avoid accusations of plagiarism. As you write up your research you will use a *citation* to indicate in your text the source of a piece of information, a paraphrase or a quotation from another work. The reader knows from the citation that you have used another author's work (you could also be citing another work of your own), and is referred to the place where full details of the source can be found. This will be in your list of references, which are normally placed at the end of your paper, dissertation, project or chapter. *References*, then, give details of books, articles and any other types of material that you have cited in your text. A *bibliography* is a list of works that you have read or consulted during the course of your research but have not necessarily cited.

Information continues to be published in an increasing variety of forms, and, as is the case with printed sources such as books, journal articles and official publications so now, standard ways are being developed to refer to documents on the Internet, the World Wide Web, or those published electronically, such as on-line journals. You can find out how to reference a wide range of publications by checking *Cite Them Right* at: http://www.unn.ac.uk/central/isd/cite/.

You may opt to create your bibliography by hand or you may prefer to use a word processor. There are also a number of bibliographic software packages available – EndNote, Pro-Cite and Reference Manager, for example – which help you to manage your information according to the rules of different referencing systems, and which prompt you to be consistent in the details you record. Some software gives you the option of importing selected bibliographic details from some on-line databases directly into the bibliography you are compiling, and in a style specified by you.

Evaluating sources

As the amount of information you collect grows and you become more experienced in your searching, you will find that you will make judgements about its value almost without thinking. It might be worth noting early on in your research the kind of questions you might apply to help you develop these evaluation skills. For example:

- Is the source you are using respected in your field?
- Has the author's name been cited by others, or have you seen it listed in other bibliographic sources?
- Are vital points referenced for you to check?
- Are the references up to date with current developments in your field?

You will soon develop a feel for your subject, but knowing that these are the kinds of criteria you are applying might save you time at the outset.

Literature searching: sources of information

You may not necessarily be able to choose to adopt the table-top/laptop approaches discussed above. Your approach will be largely dependent on the primary and secondary sources held by the library or libraries you use, and on whether you are a visitor or a registered user. Most of the printed sources mentioned in this section will be available in academic libraries, and some will be found in the larger public libraries.

Tussling with technology

For anyone who has not used computer databases, the thought of getting to grips with the new technology can be intimidating. It might help to remember that on-line sources vary widely, with differing search screens, ways of selecting and combining searches, printing out results and so on. They are changed frequently in order to become more intuitive and therefore easier to use. There are certain disadvantages to the information providers' desire to be helpful particularly if you have become familiar with the characteristics of a database. I remember only too clearly beginning a training session using a search that I had prepared the day before to demonstrate to new research staff. When I logged on, I discovered that a whole range of database interfaces had been completely redesigned, and that overnight I had become de-skilled, and was in the same position as any other first-time user. Everybody has to start somewhere though, and it is worth setting aside some time to get used to the system by trying out some trial search strategies. On-line 'Help' pages are a good place to start.

Getting to know your library

Remember to ask for help from library staff. Although most libraries produce printed guides to help their users to find their way around, talking to a librarian at the enquiry desk may help you to find out more quickly which sources and services are available to you. In particular, you will want to know where the bibliographies are, especially those in the fields of education and the social sciences. You are now using *bibliography* to mean those secondary sources – indexes and abstracts which are available on-line, or as CD-ROMs, or as microfiche, or in print versions (hard copy) – which list, by subject or country, the details of books, journal articles and so on. It is these bibliographies which you will need to use to find out what has been published on your research topic. Once you have the bibliographic details (author, title, date etc.), you can then set about obtaining the material you need to read.

You will probably start by checking the catalogue of the library you are using. Most library catalogues are on-line and probably accessible from a number of places in the library. They are often signed as OPACs and you will be guided by an on-screen menu to help you search. If the material you are looking for is not held by the library, then ask whether you are eligible to use the inter-library loan service. You will certainly be able to use the interlibrary loan service of any public library which you have joined, though bear in mind both the charges for this and the length of time that obtaining material may take.

If you are able to visit other academic libraries, and have negotiated access (for reference use for example) you can use an OPAC to check the holdings and may decide it is worth travelling elsewhere to read something you need. Laptoppers with a Web browser can check the catalogues of academic libraries on-line, without leaving their chairs, via http://www.niss.ac.uk/reference/opacs.html

The next few sections list the main sources for tracing various types of material. I have indicated whether they exist, at present, as print and/or on-line sources, to help both tabletoppers and laptoppers.

It is unusual for the design of bibliographies in hard copy to change radically, and although each differs to some extent, you will normally find notes on how to use them in the first few pages. However, it can be confusing as well as irritating to find that the *same* on-line bibliographical databases vary widely. This occurs because, although they are normally published by the same organizations that publish the printed version, access for users is usually through a service provider. Each service provider may use a standard interface for a number of different databases. Thus ERIC (Educational Resources Information Center), the main bibliographic source for finding details of journal articles and documents in education (see 'Finding journal articles', page 75) must be searched in different ways, depending on whether you are using the on-line route via the service provider BIDS (Bath Information and Data Services) or the service provider OCLC First-Search. BIDS, OCLC FirstSearch and Web of Science all provide access to on-line databases which are valuable to researchers in education and the social sciences, but users need to have registered and obtained passwords to be able to perform searches. Subscribing institutions normally pay a fee in advance which allows their staff and students unlimited access.

If you are not yet ready to begin your literature search, you may prefer to leave the following sections until you need them. You might find it more helpful at this stage to get a general idea of carrying out a search by looking instead at the section 'Literature searching: an example' (see page 81–6), which uses a small selection of the information sources available in order to find material on a particular topic.

A note on terminology

In the section 'Citations and references' (see page 69–70), I briefly defined these terms as used by those writing up a piece of research. In a wider context, 'reference' is used to mean the bibliographic details that identify a source, and some on-line service providers are using 'citation' to mean this too (e.g. ERIC via BIDS). However, the *Social Sciences Citation Index* really does index works that are cited in the text of journal articles (see below under 'Finding journal articles'). 'Index' normally refers to a bibliography that lists bibliographical details only, without 'abstracts' which additionally provide a summary of the content. As you search, you will come across sources called 'indexes' which nevertheless also include abstracts (e.g. the *British Humanities Index*).

Finding books

Using an academic library OPAC you can enter your subject keywords to find out if there are any books in your research area and whether they are in stock or out on loan. If you find any useful catalogue entries, you can note down the class numbers, then go to the shelves, and perhaps find other relevant books as you browse. You will doubtless find the publication details of other relevant material worth noting in the bibliographies of these books.

In a public library you will almost certainly be able to check the catalogue on-line. Laptoppers can find out which public libraries have on-line catalogues, and then check the holdings via http://dialspace.dial.pipex.com/town/square/ac940

To broaden your search beyond the stock of the library you are using, and to find the titles of books that have been published, or that are in print, there are some general bibliographies you can use. If you note down or print out relevant references, you can check them through the library catalogue to see whether the books are in stock. If they are not, or are out on loan, you can either put in an interlibrary loan or a recall request, or perhaps see if they are held by another library you are able to use.

American Book Publishing Record, R. R. Bowker (printed). Cumulative index to American book production.

Books in English, The British Library (microfiche). Includes all the titles that appear in the *British National Bibliography* (see below) and those catalogued by the Library of Congress.

British National Bibliography, The British Library (CD-ROM and printed). Mostly books published in the UK, but some government publications are also included.

COPAC (Consortium of University Research Libraries (CURL) Online Public Access Catalogue) (on-line via http://copac.ac.uk/copac). Unified access to the catalogues of the largest university research libraries in the UK and Ireland. Very useful for reference checking, and details may be downloaded or printed out.

Global Books in Print, Bowker Saur (CD-ROM). Includes *Books in Print* (US), *Whitaker's BookBank* (UK), *International Books in Print* (Europe, Africa, Asia, and Latin America), *Australian and New Zealand Books in Print* and *Canadian Telebank*.

Internet Bookshop (on-line via http://www.bookshop.co.uk). The records of nearly 1 million books in print in the UK. Books can be ordered on-line.

OPAC97, The British Library (on-line via http://opac97.bl.uk/). Access to 8.5 million records of material held by the British Library, including subject reference collections.

WorldCat (via OCLC FirstSearch http://firstsearch.uk.oclc.org/). A huge database of over 40 million references to books and other media held in 17,000 libraries worldwide. For book details, I rarely have to use any other source.

Finding journal articles

Abstracts and indexes give you access to thousands of references to journal articles. The frequency of publication makes journals a more fruitful up-to-date source of information than books. If you have on-line access to bibliographic databases, try these first, as they can often save you time. Often free on-line access is given by publishers and information providers to the full text of journal issues preceding the current issue, as well as access to contents pages of individual journal titles. Laptoppers might like to try http://www.scre.ac.uk/is/webjournals.html for free access to a selection of education journals and newsletters. *Ulrich's International Guide to Periodicals* (R. R. Bowker, printed) is useful for checking the full *title* of a journal (rather than an article) – especially where very similar titles exist in different countries – if, for example, you are filling out details to obtain an interlibrary loan.

Journal article subject bibliographies

British Education Index (BEI), Leeds University Press (CD-ROM – see *International ERIC*; printed and on-line via BIDS http://www.bids. ac.uk). BEI provides an index (no abstracts) to 350 British educational journals, national reports and conferences.

British Humanities Index, Bowker Saur (CD-ROM and printed). Indexes (and, from 1993, abstracts) to over 320 international newspaper and journal articles in the humanities.

Contents Pages in Education, Carfax (printed). Coverage of over 700 of the world's education journal contents pages.

Current Index to Journals in Education (CIJE), Oryx Press (printed, but see also ERIC). Provides abstracts to the articles of over 800 journals.

ERIC, US Department of Education (CD-ROM and on-line via BIDS and OCLC FirstSearch). ERIC is the largest education database, and includes both *Current Index to Journals in Education* and *Resources in Education* (RIE). RIE indexes and abstracts mainly research reports, educational documents and conferences proceedings. The ERIC computer database available via BIDS has an excellent on-line thesaurus. It is worth remembering too that many British journals indexed in the *British Education Index* (no abstracts) are also covered by ERIC, and you will therefore have access to abstracts for these articles if you use ERIC.

International Bibliography of the Social Sciences, British Library of Political and Economic Sciences, (CD-ROM, printed and on-line via BIDS). Search this for details of journal articles, book reviews and chapters from selected multi-authored works. The printed version is published as four annual volumes, each titled according to subject area: sociology, economics, political science and anthropology. Thus, you will need to look for the *International Bibliography of Sociology*, the *International Bibliography of Economics*, and so on.

International ERIC, The Dialog Corporation (CD-ROM). This CD contains the *Australian Education Index* (with abstracts) and the *British Education Index* (no abstracts).

Research into Higher Education Abstracts, Carfax on behalf of the Society for Research into Higher Education (printed). Provides a survey of international periodicals relevant to the theory and practice of higher education, with selective coverage of books and monographs.

Social Sciences Index, H. W. Wilson (CD-ROM and printed, and on-line via OCLC FirstSearch as SocSciAbs – see below). A cumulative index to English language journals in the social sciences.

Sociology of Education Abstracts, Carfax (printed). Abstracts to international sources covering theoretical, methodological and policy developments relevant to the sociological study of education.

SocSciAbs, H. W. Wilson (on-line via OCLC FirstSearch). The on-line version of the *Social Sciences Index*, but with abstracts from 1994. Covers international English language journals.

Citation index

Social Sciences Citation Index (SSCI), Institute for Scientific Information (CD-ROM, printed and on-line via Web of Science http://wos.mimas.ac.uk/). This indexes the references, or citations, that are listed at the end of journal articles. It can be useful if you want to find out who has cited articles that you have found particularly relevant to your research. You can assume that if these articles have been cited by others, then some aspect of your topic has been discussed. SSCI enables you to find full bibliographic details of the citing author's work. It is a way of tracing the future discussions or developments of a topic. You can search SSCI by subject, author, and title.

Journal articles: full text on-line

As has already been mentioned, many journal titles are available on-line, and the full text can be read on your screen, or downloaded and printed out. Some titles are published in print and electronic versions; some exist only electronically. Sometimes access is free, especially to back issues. Remember, however, that special software is often needed for reading anything other than text on screen, such as diagrams, figures or photographs.

Finding official publications

Government publications are a useful source of data, policy documents and reports for those researching in education and social science. However, tracing bibliographic details can be difficult because of the complexity of the different types of publication. Often, libraries will have a staff member who is an authority in this area, and who will be only too pleased to help. Laptoppers will probably be at an advantage in searching for and obtaining publications, because the full text of newly published reports or official statements will often be available on the Internet.

British Official Publications Current Awareness Service (BOPCAS) (http://www.soton.ac.uk/~bopcas/). This site gives up-to-date lists of official publications. Some reports can be read in full text though you must be a subscriber to do this. Details of publications from the previous six months can be browsed free.

Department for Education and Employment (DfEE) (http://www. open.gov.uk/dfee/). Outlines aims of government education policy and provides access to education statistics, reports and research findings.

Government Information Service (http://www.open.gov.uk/). Information on government departments and policies, plus the text of press releases, and general government information. There are also links to the full text of Ofsted inspection reports.

National Center for Educational Statistics (http://www.ed.gov). The

US Department of Education site for US educational programs, statistics and news.

Office for National Statistics (http://www.ons.gov.uk). UK statistics on social, economic and demographic issues.

The Stationery Office (http://the-stationery-office.co.uk/). Includes links to Acts of Parliament, and the full text of some official documents.

The Stationery Office Annual Catalogue (1996–), The Stationery Office (formerly *HMSO Annual Catalogue*, HMSO) (CD-ROM and printed). Daily, weekly and monthly printed lists are also published. The *Daily List*, and other information, is available free via http://www.the-stationery-office.co.uk/

Finding theses/research

There are a number of sources you can check if you want to know if any research is taking place or has been completed in your subject. You can obtain most dissertations and theses through purchase or interlibrary loan, and normally also consult them in the library of the institution that awarded the degree.

Current Research in Britain: Social Sciences, Cartermill International in association with the British Library (CD-ROM and printed). Details of projects, funding sources, starting and expected completion dates, plus names of those to contact for further information.

Dissertation Abstracts International, UMI Company (printed) (formerly *Dissertation Abstracts*, printed and microfiche). You will also find varying titles (*Dissertation Abstracts Online, Dissertation Abstracts Ondisc* (CD-ROM)) according to service provider or format. Contains details of advanced research, doctoral and postdoctoral. Advisable to use an electronic version if you have access, unless you have a lot of time and patience to spare.

Index to Theses with Abstracts Accepted for Higher Degrees by the Universities of Great Britain and Ireland, Aslib (printed and on-line at http://www.theses.com/). Covers all doctoral and masters theses.

You need to know the full title of this bibliography if you are look-ing it up in a library catalogue, but if you're asking in a library, then 'Aslib Index to Theses' is enough.

National Foundation for Educational Research (NFER) *Register of Educational Research*, Routledge (printed version published every two years). Aims to include completed and ongoing UK research in education and related fields, covering everything from large sponsored programmes to individual projects. Staff at NFER will search the on-line database for you for a charge. Details via http://www.nfer.ac.uk.

REGARD, Economic and Social Research Council (on-line via http://www.regard.ac.uk/). REGARD is a database containing in-depth information on social science research funded by the ESRC.

Finding Internet resources

You may wish to search beyond the few bibliographic and other good quality Internet resources mentioned above, and may already be familiar with the two Internet tools – search engines and gateways – described in this section. Often the terms 'Inter-net' and 'World Wide Web' are used interchangeably. The Internet is a huge network of networks that connects computers around the world to enable those using them to communicate. The World Wide Web ('the Web') is a part of the Internet, and consists of a collection of documents that you can move between via high-lighted links which take you to the pages/websites of the infor-mation providers. The Online Netskills Internet Course (TONIC) is a structured course offering practical guidance on major Inter-net topics for the UK higher education community (http://www.netskills.ac.uk/TONIC/).

Search engines

A search engine trawls the Web looking for documents that men-tion the keywords/index terms you have entered. The vast num-bers of search results that are sometimes achieved are not filtered in any way, and can vary widely in quality. Some search engines help to reduce the amount of dross you may have to look through by offering the option of refining your searches through the use of Boolean operators ('AND', 'OR', 'NOT'), and by giving helpful tips on strategy. It is advisable to try out several search engines until you find one or two that you know how to use well, and which bring you good quality information. For example, Alta Vista (http://www.altavista.digital.com/); Hotbot (http://www.hotbot.com/); or Metacrawler (http://www.metacrawler.com/), which simultaneously scans several search engines and produces a combined list of results ranked in order of relevance.

Internet gateways

Internet gateways guide you to collections of evaluated Internet resources which are arranged in a systematic way. Annotations can save you much time and effort by helping you to decide whether a link is worth pursuing. Two subject-specific gateways are:

NISS (National Information Systems and Services) (http://www.niss.ac.uk). The information gateway for the higher education community, which gives access to on-line databases, directories, newspapers, catalogues and reference materials.

SOSIG (Social Science Information Gateway) (http://sosig.ac.uk/). This gateway provides access to an extensive range of resources in the social sciences and education.

Literature searching: an example

Let's say that you have decided that you want to investigate the causes of mature student dropout in higher education, and you decide to find out if any research has been done on this topic in the last five years. You have set aside an afternoon to visit your university library, to do an initial search and to get a general feel about the direction that discussion in this area is taking. Your aim is to have found some useful references by the end of the afternoon, and to have some material to take away to read. You have used the library OPAC before, but only for author/title searching, you have registered to use on-line bibliographic databases but have never searched any, and you have never used printed bibliographies and have no idea where they are shelved in the library. This is the first time you have needed to do any in-depth research of your own.

Having been given some help from library staff at the enquiry desk, you now have some subject guides to bibliographic sources, a map of the library, and have found two education thesauri in the reference section. The first thesaurus has a British focus, and the second is US-focused.

Starting your keyword list (mature student dropout in higher education)

Under '**mature students**', in the *British Education Thesaurus* (1991) (2nd edn, Leeds University Press) you find that this term is used for 'non-traditional students'. There is also a lengthy list of related terms, from which you choose only 'adult students'. You reject 'university students' and 'part-time students' because they may not be mature students.

Under '**dropouts**' you choose 'adult dropouts', 'academic failure', 'academic persistence', 'attrition', 'dropout attitudes', 'dropout characteristics', 'dropout prevention', 'dropout rate', 'dropout research', 'student wastage' and 'withdrawal'. Under '**higher education**' you select 'universities' and 'colleges of higher education'.

You find nothing under 'mature students' in the *Thesaurus of ERIC Descriptors* (1995) (13th edn, Oryx Press). Instead you use '**adult students**', and under this heading you choose additionally 'adult education', 'adult learning' and 'non-traditional students'. Under '**dropouts**' you choose 'adult dropouts', 'academic persistence', 'dropout attitudes', 'dropout characteristics', 'dropout prevention', 'dropout research' and 'student attrition'. From '**higher education**', you choose only 'postsecondary education', 'colleges' and 'universities'.

Looking for books

You first try your library OPAC. You enter under the subject enquiry heading 'dropouts and mature students'. You obtain two references, one of which you want to see:

McGivney, V. (1996) *Staying or Leaving the Course: Non-completion and Retention of Mature Students in Further and Higher Education*. Leicester, National Institute of Adult Continuing Education.

The book is out on loan. You put in a reservation for it to be recalled for you.

Next you try BNB (British National Bibliography) on CD-ROM, 1986–1999. You use the index to check whether the keywords you selected from the *British Education Thesaurus* are there. You find that scrolling through the titles on-screen is so swift that you decide not to try to combine search terms. You look through all 36 entries that appear under 'dropouts'. You find the McGivney reference, but no other book title has the right focus. You print out a list, so that you can see later on which titles you rejected.

Lastly, using your username and password, you search *World-Cat*, via OCLC FirstSearch. You opt for the 'Advanced search' which allows you to refine your search by entering additional details. You can set some limits (e.g. years: 1995–2000, and only books in the English language). You use the 'browse index' option to see how many times your keywords have occurred between 1995–2000 by entering each in the 'subject (keyword)' box. 'Adult education' = 4270; 'dropouts' = 1582, 'higher education' = 10,350. In spite of this, you get no results when you combine them into one search. Perhaps you are making the focus too narrow.

You now look through the 'Help' pages and find that you can truncate your terms using a '+' in the 'subject keywords' box, but only to find plurals. This fits in with your present search, but you need to remember that truncation in OCLC FirstSearch and Web of Science is quite basic. 'School+' for example, will find the subject headings 'school' and 'schools', but not 'schooling', 'schoolteacher' or 'schoolchildren'. Thus, 'dropout+' will give you 'dropout' and 'dropouts' and any other occurrence within a phrase – 'adult education dropouts prevention' for instance. You combine this with 'higher education' as a 'subject (keyword)', perform the search and get a list of 85 records. You browse the titles, and among them once again is the McGivney reference. You know you are using the right terms therefore, but you decide that none of the other titles matches your topic. You print out the results to keep as a record. At this point, you decide that you have tried enough sources for books, and move on to finding journal articles.

Looking for journal articles

You start by searching ERIC via BIDS, because you can use BIDS to search both ERIC, the main US-oriented education database, and the main British education database, the *British Education Index*. Any British articles you find on ERIC will have abstracts, which will be useful to help you decide whether you need to read the article.

You log on, choose BIDS Education and select ERIC 1984–2000. You have already used the printed *Thesaurus of ERIC Descriptors* to make a list of keywords, which you enter in the search box. However, if you tick the 'Map Term to Subject Heading' (the on-line thesaurus) this feature automatically relates each keyword to the subject thesaurus, and allows you to choose whether to broaden or narrow your focus. You can enter also a non-thesaurus term if you prefer. 'Mature students' is not an ERIC descriptor, but still brings 74 records, because the phrase occurs in titles and abstracts which you can elect to search too. You also set some limits to your search: journal articles (CIJE) in English, between the years 1995 and 2000.

You enter your terms in your subject groupings, but find that the 'combine' feature is so easy to use that you try out a number of different permutations. You find that if you make a mistake, you can go back and re-select or delete keywords, and that you don't need a sophisticated search strategy. In the end, your 'adult students', 'dropouts' and 'higher education' sets go from a total of 30,980 records to a combined yield of 21 records. You think this is a bit low, and recombine your first two sets, but leave out the higher education set. You then display the resulting 42 records. Having read through the abstracts, you select 12 as relevant. There is a printed list of journal titles held by the library beside the computer you are using. You find that 3 of the 12 are in library stock.

One is *Adult Learning*, and you will have access straight away to: McGivney, V. 'Staying or leaving the course: non-completion and retention', *Adults Learning*, February 1996, pp. 133–135. This is a summary of some of the findings that form the basis of the 1996 McGivney book of the same title, which is out on loan from the library. The reference looks very relevant, and you are pleased that you have had the book recalled.

You next log on to *British Education Index* 1986–2000 via BIDS. You set your limits once again to the years 1995–2000. There's no on-line thesaurus. You enter each of the terms that you selected from *British Education Thesaurus* in their sets. The first set, 'mature students' or 'adult students' or 'nontraditional students' results in 171 records. Your second set on 'dropouts' is lengthy, and you are concerned that there may be a limit on the number that you can enter at one time. However, you find that the small search box expands to accept all your 12 keywords, and the search brings 121 records. Combined, these are reduced to seven. You don't bother to enter your 'higher education' set, therefore, and display all six records. Three look relevant, and are, in fact, the same three journal titles from your ERIC search that you found were in library stock. You print out the results, including the search history. As you are still in BIDS, you try out a search on *International Bibliography of the Social Sciences*, thinking it may identify some useful chapters in multi-authored/edited works, but you find nothing.

Lastly you try *Social Sciences Citation Index* via Web of Science. You log on, select 'Full Search', tick the box beside *Social Sciences Citation Index* and select the years 1995 to 2000. You could do a title or subject search, but after three hours in the library you feel you would like to find your three articles and finally get to handle some primary sources. You finish instead with a citation search by choosing the 'CITED REF SEARCH' option and entering 'McGivney' in the author box. Any authors that cite McGivney may discuss mature student dropout somewhere within their article, even if this topic is not the main focus. You find that V. McGivney has been cited 19 times, and print out the details of two articles that sound useful.

At last you can check the journal shelves. From your ERIC and BEI searches, you find the three journal articles. The McGivney summary has no references, but the digest itself is worth reading.

The second article (Frank, F. and Houghton, G. 'When life gets in the way', *Adults Learning*, May 1997, pp. 244–245) has a few references, and a contact number for further information.

The third article (Scott, C., Burns, A. and Cooney, G. 'Reasons for discontinuing study: the case of mature age female students with children', *Higher Education*, vol. 31 no. 2, March 1996, pp. 233–253) concerns an Australian study and also provides many references discussing gender issues and student dropout. It is while you are looking through this journal issue that you realize how useful it is to be able to browse. You find, by chance: Blaxter, L., Dodd, K. and Tight, M. 'Mature student markets: an institutional case study', *Higher Education*, vol. 31 no. 2, March 1996, pp. 187–203. It contains material that you feel will provide relevant background information for your study, as well as further references that you may need to follow up later.

You look at and reject one of the articles that cited McGivney, but the other (*Studies in Higher Education*, vol. 23 no. 2, June 1998, pp. 234–235) is a review by Alan Woodley of Veronica McGivney's book. Among other things, he praises her extensive literature search and the large number of institutions that provided evidence for her research. The review is authoritative and knowledgeable, and, as a consequence, you decide to make a note to find out later what Alan Woodley himself has written in this field.

You put in your interlibrary loan requests. Your list of titles for these includes:

- 'Reasons for discontinuing adult study: the case of mature-age female students with children.'
- 'The student in higher education: nontraditional student retention.'
- 'Nontraditional students: perceived barriers to degree completion.'
- 'Older coeds: predicting who will stay this time.'
- 'Adult student drop-out at post-secondary institutions.'

Finding research publications

In the printed version of *Current Research in Britain: Social Sciences* you find 'mature students' listed in the keyword index, with various aspects of the subject given alphabetically beneath, from 'access' to 'withdrawal'. You note the reference number for 'mature students – withdrawal', look up the number in the main part of the volume and find details of a research project that was undertaken between 1995 and 1996 at the University of Glasgow: Karkalas, A. M. and MacKenzie, A. *Reasons for non-completion of the Department of Adult and Continuing Education University introduction to study for mature students during three years*. You decide you will get in touch at a later date with the contacts given at the University of Glasgow to see if the project report is available.

You next turn to *Research into Higher Education Abstracts*, a printed source which you search from 1993–8. Each year has three issues, but as the third issue contains a cumulative index for the whole year you find you get through the five years very quickly. You find nothing new, but recognize many references to articles that you have already seen in other bibliographies. It is reassuring that you don't appear to have missed anything vital, and this search confirms that the same information is indexed in several different sources.

As the library subscribes to the printed edition of *Index to Theses* (see page 79–80) you are allowed access to the on-line version. You log on, and choose the 'simple search' option. You find a few titles by searching under one keyword ('dropouts') and wish to look at the full bibliographic details and abstracts. Each time you try to get the details by clicking over the title as instructed, you receive a screen full of gobbledegook. Not to be defeated, you decide to search the printed volumes from 1995–1999. It takes you almost an hour to look through the 29 printed volumes that cover these years, and although you find nothing of direct relevance, you note a couple of titles which could provide useful background reading.

However, you do learn about the vagaries of indexing – you find a thesis in one of the 1996 volumes which has 'dropout' in its title, but which has no index entry under this term. 'Adult education' is used instead. Fortunately, you were using seven keywords and 'adult education' was one of these. This re-enforces a comment you read by Alan Woodley in his McGivney review: 'statistics on non-completion are frustrating and often impenetrable, not least because of the variety of subject terms'. You have discovered, too, that the majority of research you have found on mature students focuses on their motivation, progress and performance, rather than on the causes of dropout. Woodley, in the same review, mentions McGivney's observations that institutions are coy about publicizing dropout rates. You have identified an important gap in the research on mature students.

Conclusion

By the end of your first afternoon of literature searching you have four articles to read, with relevant references from these to follow up. You have reserved a book, and put in nine interlibrary loan requests. You have also started to look into theses and research projects but will pursue these at a later date, when you've had a chance to digest all the information you've collected. You need to organize your notes and printouts, record your sources, and begin your bibliography. Now that you have planned and carried out a literature search – and made use of several bibliographies in different formats, proving yourself both a laptopper and a tabletopper – you need no longer feel a novice when you make your next library visit.

⊙ **Finding and searching information sources checklist**

1 Plan your search as soon as you can.	Decide how far back you want to search, which countries, languages, types of material you will focus on.
2 Add to your keyword list as you discover more subject terms.	Remember to note which keywords you have searched under, and which sources you have used.
3 Manage the information you retrieve.	Record bibliographic details in a systematic way, to ensure that anything you cite can be properly referenced.
4 No single bibliographic source will cover everything.	The same information will be available from different sources. Don't worry if you cannot access all the sources described. Remember too that some bibliographic sources change their titles according to the format of the material they cover: CD-ROM, on-line or hard copy.
5 If you are not retrieving anything of use, you may be using the wrong keywords or using the wrong sources.	Terminology can differ from country to country. The UK term 'educational management' becomes 'educational administration' in a US source. If your search retrieves nothing or very little from bibliographies that cover books, you may have more success when you search for journal articles.
6 Ask library staff for advice if you need any help.	

◉ 6

THE LITERATURE REVIEW

Any investigation, whatever the scale, will involve reading what other people have written about your area of interest, gathering information to support or refute your arguments and writing about your findings. In a small-scale project, you will not be expected to produce a definitive account of the state of research in your selected topic area, but you will need to provide evidence that you have read a certain amount of relevant literature and that you have some awareness of the current state of knowledge on the subject.

Ideally, the bulk of your reading should come early in the investigation, though in practice a number of activities are generally in progress at the same time and reading may even spill over into the data-collecting stage of your study. You need to take care that reading does not take up more time than can be allowed, but it is rarely possible to obtain copies of all books and articles at exactly the time you need them, so there is inevitably some overlap.

Analytical and theoretical frameworks

Reading as much as time permits about your topic may give you ideas about approach and methods which had not occurred to you and may also give you ideas about how you might classify and present your own data. It may help you to devise a theoretical or analytical framework as a basis for the analysis and interpretation of data. It is not enough merely to collect facts and to describe what is. All researchers collect many facts, but then must organize and classify them into a coherent pattern. Verma and Beard (1981) suggest that researchers need to

> identify and explain relevant relationships between the facts. In other words, the researcher must produce a concept or build a theoretical structure that can explain facts and the relationships between them . . . The importance of theory is to help the investigator summarize previous information and guide his future course of action. Sometimes the formulation of a theory may indicate missing ideas or links and the kinds of additional data required. Thus, a theory is an essential tool of research in stimulating the advancement of knowledge still further.
>
> (Verma and Beard 1981: 10)

Sometimes 'model' is used instead of or interchangeably with 'theory'. Cohen and Manion explain that

> both may be seen as explanatory devices or schemes having a conceptual framework, though models are often characterized by the use of analogies to give a more graphic or visual representation of a particular phenomenon. Providing they are accurate and do not misrepresent the facts, models can be of great help in achieving clarity and focusing on key issues in the nature of phenomena.
>
> (Cohen and Manion 1994: 16)

The label is not important but the process of ordering and classifying data is.

As you read, get into the habit of examining how authors classify their findings, how they explore relationships between facts and how facts and relationships are explained. Methods used by other researchers may be unsuitable for your purposes, but they may give you ideas about how you might categorize your own data, and ways in which you may be able to draw on the work of other researchers to support or refute your own arguments and conclusions.

The critical review of the literature

An extensive study of the literature will be required in most cases for a PhD and a critical review of what has been written on the topic produced in the final thesis. A project lasting two or three months will not require anything so ambitious. You may decide to omit an initial review altogether if your reading has not been sufficiently extensive to warrant its inclusion, but if you decide to produce a review, it is important to remember that only relevant works are mentioned and that the review is more than a list of 'what I have read'.

Writing literature reviews can be a demanding exercise. Haywood and Wragg comment wryly that critical reviews are more often than not uncritical reviews – what they describe as

> the furniture sale catalogue, in which everything merits a one-paragraph entry no matter how skilfully it has been conducted: Bloggs (1975) found this, Smith (1976) found that, Jones (1977) found the other, Bloggs, Smith and Jones (1978) found happiness in heaven.
>
> (Haywood and Wragg 1982: 2)

Blaxter *et al.* (1996b: 115) provide us with useful reminders about the uses and abuses of references. They suggest that you should use references to:

- justify and support your arguments;
- allow you to make comparisons with other research;
- express matters better than you could have done;
- demonstrate your familiarity with your field of research.

They also suggest that you should not use references to:

- impress your readers with the scope of your reading;
- litter your writing with names and quotations;

- replace the need for you to express your own thoughts;
- misrepresent other authors.

(Blaxter *et al*. 1996b: 115)

It requires discipline to produce a critical review which demonstrates 'that the writer has studied existing work in the field with insight' (Haywood and Wragg 1982: 2), but the main point to bear in mind is that a review should provide the reader with a picture, albeit limited in a short project, of the state of knowledge and of major questions in the subject area being investigated.

Consider the following introduction to a study by Alan Woodley (1985) entitled 'Taking account of mature students'. You may not be familiar with this field of study, but does the introduction put you in the picture? Does it give you some idea of the work that has been done already and does it prepare you for what is to follow?

Of the many who have looked at the relationship between age and performance in universities none has as yet produced a definite answer to the apparently simple question 'Do mature students do better or worse than younger students?'

Harris (1940) in the United States found evidence to suggest that younger students tended to obtain better degree results. Similar findings have been made in Britain by Malleson (1959), Howell (1962), Barnett and Lewis (1963), McCracken (1969) and Kapur (1972), in Australia by Flecker (1959) and Sanders (1961), in Canada by Fleming (1959), and in New Zealand by Small (1966). However, most of these studies were based on samples of students who were generally aged between seventeen and twenty-one and the correlation techniques employed meant that the relationships between age and performance really only concerned this narrow age band. As such, the results probably suggest that bright children admitted early to higher education fare better than those whose entry is delayed while they gain the necessary qualifications. This view is supported by Harris (1940) who discovered that the relationship between age and performance disappeared when he controlled for intelligence. Other studies have shown that those who gain the necessary qualifications and then delay entry for a year or two are more successful than those who enter directly from school (Thomas, Beeby and Oram 1939; Derbyshire Education Committee 1966).

Where studies have involved samples containing large numbers of older students the results have indicated that the relationship between age and performance is not a linear one. Philips and Cullen (1955), for instance, found that those aged twenty-four and over tended to do better than the eighteen and nineteen-year-old age group. Sanders (1961) showed that the university success rate fell until the age of twenty or twenty-one, then from about twenty-two onwards the success rate began to rise again. The problem with these two studies is that many of the older students were returning servicemen. They were often 'normal' entrants whose entry to university had been delayed by war and many had undergone some training in science or mathematics while in the armed forces. Also, while Eaton (1980) cites nine American studies which confirm the academic superiority of veterans, there is some contradictory British evidence. Mountford (1957) found that ex-service students who entered Liverpool University between 1947 and 1949 were more likely to have to spend an extra year or more on their courses and more likely to fail to complete their course.

Some studies have shown that whether mature students fare better or worse than younger students depends upon the subject being studied. Sanders (1963) has indicated that the maturity associated with increasing age and experience seems to be a positive predictor of success for some arts and social science courses. The general finding that older students do better in arts and social science and worse in science and maths is supported by Flecker (1959), Barnett, Holder and Lewis (1968), Fagin (1971) and Sharon (1971).

Walker's (1975) study of mature students at Warwick University represents the best British attempt to unravel the relationship between age and performance. He took 240 mature undergraduates who were admitted to the university between 1965 and 1971 and compared their progress with that of all undergraduates. This gave him a reasonably large sample to work with and the timing meant that the results were not distorted by any 'returning servicemen factor'. His methodology showed certain other refinements. First, he excluded overseas students. Such students tend to be older than average and also to fare worse academically (Woodley 1979), thus influencing any age/performance relationship. Secondly, he used two measures of performance; the proportion leaving without obtaining a degree and the degree results of those taking final examinations. Finally he weighted the degree class obtained according to its rarity value in each faculty.

The following findings achieved statistical significance:

(i) In total, mature students obtained better degrees than non-mature students.

(ii) In the arts faculty mature students obtained better degrees than non-mature students.

(iii) Mature students who did not satisfy the general entrance requirements obtained better degrees than all other students.

(iv) The degree results of mature students aged twenty-six to thirty were better than those of all other mature students.

Several other differences were noted but they did not achieve statistical significance due to the small numbers involved. The mature student sample only contained thirty-three women, twenty-six science students and thirty-seven aged over thirty. The aim of the present study was to extend Walker's work to all British universities so that these and other relationships could be tested out on a much larger sample of mature students.

(Woodley 1985: 152–4)

This review is more thorough than would normally be required for small projects, but the approach is much the same, whatever the exercise. Alan Woodley selects from the extensive amount of literature relating to mature students. He groups certain categories and comments on features which are of particular interest. He compares results of different investigators and discusses in some detail a study by Walker (1975) which serves as a pilot for his more extensive study of mature students in British universities.

The reader is then in the picture and has some understanding of what work has been done already in this field. Woodley no doubt omitted many publications that had been consulted during the course of his research. It is always hard to leave out publications that may have taken many hours or even weeks to read, but the selection has to be made. That is the discipline which has to be mastered. Once you have identified possible categories from your initial reading, and have your cards and/or computer references and notes in order, you will be able to group the source material, and writing the review becomes much easier.

A second example of a successful literature review, this time relating to an MEd dissertation, was produced by Clara Nai, a Singaporean-based MEd student of the University of Sheffield. She was investigating barriers to what she described as continuous learning amongst mature workers at Singapore airport. She discussed in some detail her own methodology, the methodology used by other researchers and the problems she faced in synthesizing the very large amount of information obtained about barriers to learning. She had read a great deal and faced the usual difficulties in grouping what she felt to be significant research findings. She writes:

> Having read so much, it took me a while to reconcile what I can present in a condensed review. It seems so unfair that only a fraction of the months of painstaking reading could appear in print. Putting sentiments aside, I have decided . . . to classify the factors affecting participation under some major headings for ease of consolidation.
>
> (Nai 1996: 33)

I imagine a good many new and experienced researchers will sympathize with Clara's exasperation. Identifying categories early in reading helps, even if some have to be rejected and others added, but if no attempt has been made, then deciding on categories becomes very difficult *and* extremely time-consuming. Clara sensibly examined the way other researchers had categorized their findings and decided to use the broad grouping into situational, institutional and dispositional barriers to learning adopted by Cross (1981). There is no reason why researchers should not adopt a methodology devised by someone else, as Alan Woodley proposed to do in the first example, as long as the source is acknowledged.

The choice of headings worked well. There is insufficient space here to reproduce the full review, but I hope the following extract from Clara's 'Institutional barriers' section gives an idea of the way she approached the task.

> Institutional barriers rank second in importance after situational barriers, accounting for between 10 to 25% of potential learners among respondents in most surveys (Cross, 1981). They are policies and procedures usually unintentionally put up by policymakers, human resource personnel or educational providers.
>
> Cross has grouped institutional barriers under 'scheduling problems', 'location/transportation problems', 'lack of interesting, practical or relevant courses', 'procedural registration problems', 'strict admission criteria' and 'lack of information'. Of these, up to a quarter cited inconvenient locations, inconvenient scheduling and the lack of interesting or relevant courses as the greatest barriers to participation. Ten per cent of British workers specified 'a lack of suitable courses' as an obstacle (Great Britain Training Agency, 1989: Table 11.21).
>
> The open university concept, of which UK's British Open University, Open Tech, Open Learning and Open College are good examples of initiatives designed specifically for working adults, is surprisingly fraught with institutional barriers. McIntosh and Woodley (1975) made some observations of the obstacles confronting candidates of the British Open University. The study shows that unless administrators of these learning institutions are willing to substantially compromise standards, the elimination of barriers will remain a dream. For example, are open learning institutions willing to grant mothers with young children exemption from compulsory attendance, lower minimal passed grades for the lowly

educated, waive tuition fees for the economically disadvantaged or re-schedule classes to accommodate shift-workers?

Indeed, the survey of higher education sponsored by the US Commission on Non-Traditional Study (Ruyle and Geiselman, 1974) shows that colleges are already re-scheduling classes, granting credit by examination for non-collegiate learning and creating flexible admissions procedures – with the adult student in mind. Yet, many adults still face insurmountable obstacles in participating.

(Nai 1996: 35–6)

Does this extract begin to provide you with some background to the problem of institutional barriers, as identified in the four quoted sources? A great deal more could have been included, but this was an MEd dissertation, not a PhD and an MEd literature review is not expected to present the definitive account of all the research that has ever been published in this area. Literature reviews have to be succinct and it will never be possible or desirable to include everything that has been read. As Clara discovered, it may well be that a great deal of what has been read will need to be abandoned when the review is prepared. What at one stage might have seemed to be a promising line of enquiry may prove to be of little use once more reading has been done. A hundred, or even a thousand individual pieces of information may emerge and be interesting in their own right but it is only when they are grouped, balanced against other findings and presented in a way readers can understand, that you have a review which is coherent and which has avoided the 'furniture sale catalogue' approach. All this requires disciplined recording of source material *from the beginning of your research* and as your reading develops, taking note of likely keywords, categories and groupings.

 **Part II**

SELECTING METHODS OF
DATA COLLECTION

INTRODUCTION

When you have decided on a topic, refined it and specified objectives, you will be in a position to consider how to collect the evidence you require. The initial question is not 'Which methodology?' but 'What do I need to know and why?' Only then do you ask 'What is the best way to collect information?' and 'When I have this information, what shall I do with it?'

No approach depends solely on one method any more than it would exclude a method merely because it is labelled 'quantitative', 'qualitative', 'case study', 'action research', or whatever. As I indicated in Chapter 1, some approaches depend heavily on one type of data-collecting method – but not exclusively. You may consider that a study making use of a questionnaire will inevitably be quantitative, but it may also have qualitative features. Case studies, which are generally considered to be qualitative studies, can combine a wide range of methods, including quantitative techniques. Methods are selected because they will provide the data you require to produce a complete piece of research. Decisions have to be made about which methods are best for particular purposes and then data-collecting instruments must be designed to do the job.

Constraints

The extent of your data-collecting will be influenced by the amount of time you have. This may seem a rather negative approach, but there is no point in producing a grandiose scheme that requires a year and a team of researchers if you are on your own, have no funds and in any case have to hand in the project report in three months. Even so, if possible, efforts should be made to cross-check findings, and in a more extensive study, to use more than one method of data-collecting. This multi-method approach is known as *triangulation*, and is described in Open University course E811 as

> cross-checking the existence of certain phenomena and the veracity of individual accounts by gathering data from a number of informants and a number of sources and subsequently comparing and contrasting one account with another in order to produce as full and balanced a study as possible.
>
> (Open University course E811 1988: 54)

Cohen and Manion (1994: 240) take the issue of triangulation a stage further:

> Multiple methods are suitable where a controversial aspect of education needs to be evaluated more fully. The issue of comprehensive schools, for example, has been hotly debated since their inception; yet even at this point there has been little serious research investigating these institutions as totalities. It is not sufficient to judge these schools solely on the grounds of academic achievement with 'league tables' based on O and A level results, important as these are. A much more rounded portrayal of these institutions is required and here is a clear case for the advocacy of multiple methods.

They suggest that multiple methods could measure and investigate factors such as 'academic achievements, teaching methods, practical skills, cultural interests, social skills, interpersonal relationships, community spirit and so on'. In longer term research, 'validity could then be greatly increased by researching a large sample of schools (space triangulation) once a year say, over a period of five years (time triangulation)' (p. 240).

Longer-term research of this kind is likely to produce rich findings, but no 100-hour project student and few PhD researchers would have the luxury of five years of follow-up studies. Most 100-hour projects would be limited to single method studies. You just do the best you can *in the available time*. There are likely to be other constraints. For example, if you wish to observe meetings, you will be limited by the number and timing of meetings that are scheduled to take place in the period of your study. The willingness of people to be interviewed or observed, to complete the questionnaire or diaries will inevitably affect your decisions as to which instruments to use. You may feel that a postal questionnaire would be the most suitable method of obtaining certain information, but postal questionnaires can cost quite a lot of money, so you will have to consider whether funds can be found – and whether this expenditure will be worthwhile.

Reliability and validity

Whatever procedure for collecting data is selected, it should always be examined critically to assess to what extent it is likely to be reliable and valid. *Reliability* is the extent to which a test or procedure produces similar results under constant conditions on all occasions. A clock which runs ten minutes slow some days and fast on other days is unreliable. A factual question which may produce one type of answer on one occasion but a different answer on another is equally unreliable. Questions which ask for opinions may produce different answers for a whole range of reasons. The respondent may just have seen a television programme which affected opinions or may have had some experience which angered or pleased and so affected response. Wragg (1980: 17), writing about interviews, asks: 'Would two interviewers using the schedule or procedure get a similar result? Would an interviewer obtain a similar picture using the procedures on different occasions?' These are reasonable questions to put to yourself when you check items on a questionnaire or interview schedule.

There are numbers of devices for checking reliability in scales and tests, such as *test-retest* (administering the same test some time after the first), the *alternate forms method* (where equivalent versions of the same items are given and results correlated) or the *split-half method* (where the items in the test are split into two matched halves and scores then correlated). These methods are not always feasible or necessary, and there are disadvantages and problems associated with all three. Generally, unless your supervisor advises otherwise, such checking mechanisms will not be necessary unless you are attempting to produce a test or scale. The check for reliability will come at the stage of question wording and piloting of the instrument.

Validity is an altogether more complex concept. It tells us whether an item measures or describes what it is supposed to measure or describe. If an item is unreliable, then it must also lack validity, but a reliable item is not necessarily also valid. It could produce the same or similar responses on all occasions, but not be measuring what it is supposed to measure. This seems straightforward enough, but measuring the extent of validity can become extremely involved, and there are many variations and subdivisions of validity. For the purpose of 100-hour projects that are not concerned with complex testing and measurement, it is rarely necessary to delve deeply into the measurement of validity, though efforts should be made to examine items critically.

Ask yourself whether another researcher using your research instrument would be likely to get the same responses. Tell other people (colleagues, pilot respondents, fellow students) what you are trying to find out or to measure and ask them whether the questions or items you have devised are likely to do the job. This rough-and-ready method will at least remind you of the need to achieve some degree of reliability and validity in question wording, even though it is unlikely to satisfy researchers involved with administering scales and tests with large numbers of subjects.

It is often worrying for first-time researchers to know how many questionnaires should be distributed or interviews given. There are no set rules, and you should ask for guidance from your supervisor before you commit yourself to a grand plan that will be far in excess of what is required. Your aim is to obtain as representative a range of responses as possible to enable you to fulfil the objectives of your study and to provide answers to key questions.

Research instruments are selected and devised to enable you to obtain these answers. The instrument is merely the tool to enable you to gather data, and it is important to select the best tool for the job. The following chapters take you through the processes involved in the analysis of documentary evidence, designing and administering questionnaires, planning and conducting interviews, diaries and observation studies. Little attention is given to analysis of data in this part, but all data have to be analysed and interpreted to be of any use, and so Chapters 12 and 13 in Part III should be studied in association with the chapters in Part II.

Further reading

The sources mentioned in this Introduction to Part II are all sound and merit further study. The following also provide guidance.

Hammersley, M. (1987) 'Some notes on the terms "validity" and "reliability"', *British Educational Research Journal*, 13(1), 73–81. This very comprehensive review discusses the meaning of reliability and validity and comments on inconsistencies in definition and application. A scholarly piece of work, but a hard read.

Kirk, J. and Miller, M.L. (1985) *Reliability and Validity in Qualitative Research*. California: Sage. Discusses issues relating to the qualitative/quantitative debate and makes the case for greater reliability and validity in qualitative studies.

7

THE ANALYSIS OF DOCUMENTARY EVIDENCE

Brendan Duffy

Most educational projects will require the analysis of documentary evidence. In some, it will be used to supplement information obtained by other methods, as for instance when the reliability of evidence gathered from interviews or questionnaires is checked. In others, it will be the central or even exclusive method of research. It will be particularly useful when access to the subjects of research is difficult or impossible as in the case where a longitudinal study is undertaken and staff members no longer belong to the organization being investigated. The lack of access to research subjects may be frustrating, but documentary analysis of educational files and records can prove to be an extremely valuable alternative source of data (Johnson 1984: 23). This chapter aims to explain how to locate, categorize, select and analyse documents. Its approach is derived from historical methods which are essentially concerned with the problems of selection and evaluation of evidence. Such methods were first developed by Von Ranke and have influenced the form of all academic report writing (Barzun and Graff 1977: 5; Evans 1997: 18).

Approaches to documents

When embarking on a study using documents it is possible to have two different approaches. One has been called the 'source-oriented' approach in which you let the nature of the sources determine your project and help you generate questions for your research. You would not bring predetermined questions to the sources but would be led by the material they contain. The second and more common approach would be the 'problem-oriented approach' which involves formulating questions by reading *secondary sources*, reading what has already been discovered about the subject and establishing the focus of the study before going to the relevant *primary sources* (these terms are defined below). As your research progresses a much clearer idea of which sources are relevant will emerge and more questions will occur to you as your knowledge of the subject deepens (Tosh 1991: 54).

The location of documents

Document searches need to be carried out in exactly the same way as literature searches in order to assess whether your proposed project is feasible and to inform yourself about the background to, and the nature of, the subject. The document search may have to cover both national and local sources of evidence.

At the local level, the nature of the project will lead you to particular sources. A project on the relationship between a college and its funding body would require a document search of the records of both institutions, and account would have to be taken of their special characteristics. If the college had an academic board or equivalent, its minutes would be one source; if the funding authority's departments dealt with different aspects of the college's administration, their records would be significant. It is important to inquire as to what archives or collections of records exist in an organization. What records are preserved by the school office, the bursar (or financial officer) or the library, and what records may be stored by individuals or departments in the institution? Does the local education authority hold records for particular schools? How long do organizations hold onto records before they dispose of them? Researchers can be frustrated by the official weeding policy of government departments which may have resulted in the destruction of sources later discovered to be significant (Duffy 1998: 29–30). As a researcher you must be prepared to hunt down sources of information. It can never be assumed, of course, that because documents exist they will be available for research. Some sources may be regarded as too confidential to be released, so enquiries would have to be made about access and availability.

The nature of documentary evidence

During the document search it is helpful to clarify exactly what kinds of documents exist. 'Document' is a general term for an impression left on a physical object by a human being. Research can involve the analysis of photographs, films, videos, slides and other non-written sources, all of which can be classed as documents, but the most common kinds of documents in educational research are written as printed sources, so this chapter concentrates on these. Sources can also be quantitative or statistical in nature but it would be a mistake, of course, to regard these so-called 'hard' sources of evidence as being more reliable than other kinds of material. It is vitally important to employ the recommended critical method of analysis to check how the figures have been produced. What has been counted? How correctly? By whom? When? Where? And why? (Stanford 1994: 146).

Primary and secondary sources

Documents can be divided into primary and secondary sources. *Primary sources* are those which came into existence in the period under research (e.g. the minutes of a school's governors' meetings). *Secondary sources* are interpretations of events of that period based on primary sources (e.g. a history of that school which obtained evidence from the governors' minutes). The distinction is complicated by the fact that some documents are primary from one point of view and secondary from another (Marwick 1989:

200). If the author of the school history was the subject of research, for example, her or his book would become a primary source for the researcher. The term '*secondary analysis*', used by some social scientists (Hakim 1982) to mean the analysis of survey material or primary documents gathered in collections, is not helpful because it can be confused with the use of secondary sources. Such secondary analysis is, of course, primary research as defined here.

Deliberate and inadvertent sources

Primary sources can in turn be divided into two categories. *Deliberate sources* are produced for the attention of future researchers. These would include autobiographies, memoirs of politicians or educationalists, diaries or letters intended for later publication and documents of self-justification (Elton 1967: 101). They involve a deliberate attempt to preserve evidence for the future, possibly for purposes of self-vindication or reputation enhancement (Lehmann and Mehrens 1971: 24).

Inadvertent sources are used by the researcher for some purpose other than that for which they were originally intended. They are produced by the processes of local and central government and from the everyday working of the education system. Examples of such primary documents are:

- the records of legislative bodies, government departments and local education authorities;
- evidence from national databases;
- inspection reports;
- national surveys;
- the minutes of academic boards, senior management groups, middle management meetings, working groups and staff meetings;
- handbooks and prospectuses;
- examination papers;
- attendance registers;
- personal files;
- staffing returns;

- option-choice documents;
- bulletins;
- letters and newspapers;
- budget statements;
- school or college websites and other Internet material.

Such inadvertent documents are the more common and usually the more valuable kind of primary sources. They were produced for a contemporary practical purpose and would therefore seem to be more straightforward than deliberate sources. This may be the case, but great care still needs to be taken with them because it cannot be discounted that inadvertent documents were intended to deceive someone other than the researcher, or that what first appear to be inadvertent sources (some government records, for example) are actually attempts to justify actions to future generations (Elton 1967: 102). Some of the documents generated by a school for an inspection may have the aim of giving the best possible impression on the inspectors, and the school might not be so prolific in its production of policy statements or so up to date in its handbook if the inspection was not imminent.

Witting and unwitting evidence

A final point about the nature of documents concerns their 'witting' and 'unwitting' evidence. *Witting* evidence is the information which the original author of the documents wanted to impart. *Unwitting* evidence is everything else that can be learned from the document (Marwick 1989: 216). If, for example, a government minister made a speech announcing a proposed educational reform, the witting evidence would be everything that was stated in the speech about the proposed change. The unwitting evidence, on the other hand, might come from any underlying assumptions unintentionally revealed by the minister in the language he or she used, and from the fact that a particular method had been chosen by the government to announce the reform. If a junior minister is given the job of announcing a reduction in educational expenditure it may well indicate the expectation on the part of more senior colleagues that the government will be criticized.

All documents provide unwitting evidence, but it is the task of the researcher to try to assess its precise significance.

The selection of documents

The amount of documentary material that you can study will inevitably be influenced by the amount of time that is available for this stage of your research. It is not usually possible to analyse everything, so you must decide what to select. Familiarity with the different categories of evidence will help you to make decisions about what is fundamental to the project, and 'controlled selection' is then needed to ensure that no significant category is left out (Elton 1967: 92). Try not to include too many deliberate sources and take care not to select documents merely on the basis of how well they support your own views or hypotheses. Your aim is to make as balanced a selection as possible, bearing in mind the constraints of time. Periodically, check with your schedule, and if you find that you are encroaching on time allocated for the next stage of your research, take steps to reduce your selection. Your perception of what is valuable will grow as the project develops.

Content analysis

The proper selection of documents is particularly important in what is termed 'content analysis' which has been defined as 'a research technique for making replicable and valid inferences from data to their context' (Krippendorff 1980: 21). Content analysis has been used to analyse bias in news reporting, the content of newspapers, the extent of sexual or racial stereotypes in textbooks, the differences in black and white popular song lyrics and the nationalist bias in history textbooks (Weber 1990: 10). It usually involves counting the number of times particular terms or 'recording units' occur in a sample of sources but it could also involve such methods as counting the number of column inches devoted to a subject in a newspaper or the number of photographs in a publication. It might be possible to study all the documents in a particular category such as school newsletters or prospectuses but in other cases a sampling technique is needed. Such an example would be if a daily newspaper is selected in a research project investigating tabloid newspapers' attitudes to comprehensive schools. You could examine all the editions of a newspaper over a three-month period or you could take the first week in each month over a one-year period. The nature of the sample must be able to be defended and it must be sufficiently large to allow valid conclusions. If the researcher was interested in the media presentation of teachers' associations, the sampling of newspapers from the first week of each month would be very inappropriate because significant references to specific associations are unlikely to be confined to the first week of each month. Having established the frequency of your chosen terms you must then be able to place them in context before interpreting and explaining them. In order to do that successfully it is necessary to apply the critical method advocated in the next section. Content analysis of documents can be very arid in its approach if the nature of the documents is not analysed in the way suggested here, and it may not be appropriate for many small-scale studies.

The critical analysis of documents

External criticism

The analysis of documents can be divided into external and internal *criticism*, even though these may overlap to a large extent. *External criticism* aims to discover whether a document is both genuine (i.e. not forged) and authentic (i.e. it is what it purports to be and truthfully reports on its subject) (Barzun and Graff 1977: 85). For example, observers could write a report of a meeting they had never attended. Their report would be genuine, because they actually wrote it, but it would not be authentic because they were not present at the meeting.

In external criticism it is necessary to know for certain that the author produced the document, so certain questions need to be asked. In the case of a letter, they would include the following:

- Was the author of the letter known to be in the place from which it came at the time it was written?
- Do other sources corroborate that the person wrote the letter? Is the letter consistent with all other facts known about the author?
- Does it use the same arrangements and have the same form as similar documents?
- Is it typical of other letters or documents written by the author?

It is unlikely that you will need or be able to verify any forgeries or hoaxes but an attempt should be made to decide whether a person did actually compose the speech delivered or write the letter with her or his signature on it.

Internal criticism

The analytical method more likely to be used in small-scale educational research is *internal criticism*, in which the contents of a document are subjected to rigorous analysis which first seeks answers to the following questions:

- What kind of document is it? A government circular? A statute? A policy paper? A set of minutes? A letter from a long correspondence? How many copies are there?
- What does it actually say? Are the terms used employed in the same way as you would use them? Documents such as statutes or legal papers may employ a specialized language which must be mastered, and private correspondence may use terms in an idiosyncratic way that also needs to be understood.
- Who produced it? What is known about the author?
- What was its purpose? Did the author aim to inform, command, remind (as in a memorandum) or to have some other effect on the reader? A document is always written for a particular readership and shaped according to the writer's expectations of how intended readers will interpret it (Evans 1997: 104). In the same way, the reader is always conscious of the purposes and intentions of the writer during the act of reading.

- When and in what circumstances was it produced? How did it come into existence?
- Is it typical or exceptional of its type?
- Is it complete? Has it been altered or edited? It may be that there is more chance of completeness if it was published a long time after the events it describes.

You will also need to assess the assiduousness of the producers of documents. Staff will complete documents very carefully if they are to be used in appeals procedures or public meetings and their approach to reporting on a pupil will be different if they know that the pupil's parents and others will see the document rather than just their colleagues.

After asking these basic questions, you will need to ask further questions about the author:

- What is known about the author's social background, political views, aims and past experience?
- Did the author experience or observe what is being described? If so, was he or she an expert on what was being witnessed and a trained observer of the events described?
- Did the author habitually tell the truth or exaggerate, distort or omit?
- How long after the event did the author produce the document? Is it possible that memory played tricks?

All these questions may not be relevant to all documents, but in aiming at critical analysis it is important not to accept sources at face value. Examine them carefully. Gaps in the evidence can sometimes be very significant as they may indicate a prejudice or a determination to ignore a proposed change. Decide whether a particular political affiliation might possibly influence the tone or emphasis of a paper and try to come to a conclusion based on all the available evidence. An assessment of the document's reliability must involve the question: 'Reliable for what?' Is it a reliable explanation of the author's views on an issue? In other words, is it representative of those views? It might not be truthful in a more general sense – for example, a document supporting streaming in schools may not necessarily convey the truth about the effects of using this method of organizing classes in a school, but it would be a truthful and therefore reliable expression of the author's views on the subject. Alternatively the source might be a reliable example of its type, as in the case of a document from a long series.

Fact or bias?

One important aim of critical scholarship is to assess whether fact or bias is the main characteristic of a document (Barzun and Graff 1977: 154). Writers will rarely declare their assumptions, so it is the task of the researcher to expose them if possible. Watch particularly for any terms that suggest partisanship. Ask yourself whether the evidence supplied in the document convincingly supports the author's arguments. Was the author a supporter of a particular course of action in which he or she had a stake? If the document goes against the author's own interest, it may increase the likelihood that it tells the truth. Was the author affected by pressure, fear or even vanity when writing the document? (Best 1970: 105). Look for *clues*.

If you detect bias, this does not necessarily mean that the document should be dismissed as worthless. In some cases the most useful evidence can be derived from biased sources which reveal accurately the true views of an individual or group. Inferences can still be drawn from the unwitting testimony, even if the witting evidence is thought to be unsound. A prejudiced account of curriculum development, for example, could provide valuable insights into the political processes involved in innovation. The biased document will certainly need to be analysed cautiously and compared with evidence from other sources, but it can still be valuable.

Try to stand in the position of the author of the document and to see through her or his eyes. Instead of jumping to early conclusions, deliberately seek contrary evidence to test the truthfulness of a document as rigorously as possible – and watch out for your own bias. It may be easier to recognize bias in others than it is to recognize it in ourselves, and it is tempting to reject evidence that does not support our case. Try to resist the temptation.

Sources can be interpreted in different ways (even though some sources can reasonably be understood in only one way) but the postmodernist view that documents can be subjected to an infinity of meaning has been brilliantly demolished by Evans (1997). The guiding principle in document analysis is nevertheless that everything should be questioned. Qualities of scepticism as well as empathy need to be developed.

It could be argued that the techniques of document analysis suggested here are merely the application of common sense (Tosh 1991: 71). This is partly true, but as you study the sources you will gradually gain insights and detailed knowledge which will give you a 'higher common sense' which will in turn permit a fuller appreciation of the worth of the evidence (Barzun and Graff 1977: 130). Eventually, the critical method becomes a habit which will allow you, in Marwick's phrase, to 'squeeze the last drop' from each document (Marwick 1989: 233).

⊙ The analysis of documentary evidence checklist

1	Decide how you want to use documentary evidence.	Will it be used to supplement other sources of evidence or will you use it as the exclusive method of gathering data?
2	Decide on your approach to the documents.	You can let the source material determine your research questions or, more commonly, you will formulate your research questions after reading the literature on the subject and take these questions to the sources.
3	Undertake a document search to ascertain the existence of different sources of information.	Documents may be found in different places in an organization so it is important to be persistent. Always negotiate access to the documents and do not assume that you can consult them; some information may be confidential.
4	Analyse the nature of the sources used.	Some sources will be deliberately produced for the attention of

future researchers but, more usually, sources will be inadvertently produced by the everyday working of the education system.

5 If the documents are bulky it may be necessary to decide on a sampling strategy.

Try to read a balanced selection of documents in the time you have available. The strategy must be appropriate to the purposes of your research and be capable of being justified in your report.

6 Be aware that there may be different kinds of evidence in each document.

Look for witting and unwitting evidence.

7 Subject each document to the critical method and ask a range of questions.

What does it say? Who wrote it? Why? How did it come into existence? Is it typical of its kind? Is it complete?

8 Compare the document with other sources to see if it is accurate or representative.

9 Then ask further questions about the authors of documents.

What is their background and social and political views? Did they experience or observe what they are writing about? Did they usually tell the truth?

10 Detect bias in the document.

Remember that biased evidence can be very valuable.

11 Decide whether the document is reliable for a particular purpose.

Check it against other sources to ascertain its truthfulness but remember that although it may not be an accurate account of an event or development, it may be a reliable expression of the author's views.

12 Strive to gain a full appreciation of the value of a source.

Use your accumulating knowledge to gain insights and try to make the critical method a habit in your research methods.

8

DESIGNING
AND ADMINISTERING
QUESTIONNAIRES

You will only reach the stage of designing a questionnaire after you have done all the preliminary work on planning, consulting and deciding exactly what you need to find out. Only then will you know whether a questionnaire is suitable for the purpose and likely to yield usable data. Ask yourself whether a questionnaire is likely to be a better way of collecting information than interviews or observation, for example. If it is, then you will need to ensure you produce a well-designed questionnaire that will give you the information you need, that will be acceptable to your subjects and that will give you no problems at the analysis and interpretation stage.

It is harder to produce a really good questionnaire than might be imagined. Oppenheim (1966: vii), in the Preface to his book *Questionnaire Design and Attitude Measurement*, wrote that 'the world is full of well meaning people who believe that anyone who can write plain English and has a modicum of common sense can produce a good questionnaire'. He goes on to demonstrate that though common sense and the ability to write plain English will help, that will not be sufficient. Care has to be taken in selecting question type, in question-writing, in the design, piloting, distribution and return of questionnaires. Thought must be given to how responses will be analysed at the design stage, not after all the questionnaires have been returned. Questionnaires are a good way of collecting certain types of information quickly and relatively cheaply as long as you are sufficiently disciplined to abandon questions that are superfluous to the main task.

Exactly what do you need to find out?

Your preliminary reading and your research plan will have identified important areas for investigation. Go back to your hypothesis or to the objectives and decide which questions you need to ask to achieve these objectives. Then write out possible questions on cards or on separate pieces of paper, to aid ordering at a later stage. You will need several attempts at wording in order to remove ambiguity, to achieve the degree of precision necessary to ensure that subjects understand exactly what you are asking, to check that your language is jargon free, to decide which question type to use and to ensure that you will be able to classify and analyse responses. Guidance about analysis is provided in Chapter 12, and before you complete your questionnaire design you should read this chapter carefully. Time spent on preparation will save many hours of work later on.

Question type

The more structured a question, the easier it will be to analyse. Youngman (1986) lists seven question types as follows:

| Verbal or Open | The expected response is a word, a phrase or an extended comment. Responses to verbal questions can produce useful information but analysis can present problems. Some form of content analysis may be required for verbal material unless the information obtained is to be used for special purposes. For example, you might feel it necessary to give respondents the opportunity to give their own views on the topic being researched – or to raise a |

grievance. You might wish to use questions as an introduction to a follow-up interview, or in pilot interviews where it is important to know which aspects of the topic are of particular importance to the respondents.

More structured questions will not present so many problems at the analysis stage. Youngman suggests the following:

List
: A list of items is offered, any of which may be selected. For example, a question may ask about qualifications and the respondent may have several of the qualifications listed.

Category
: The response is one only of a given set of categories. For example, if age categories are provided (20–29, 30–39, etc.), the respondent can only fit into one category.

Ranking
: In ranking questions, the respondent is asked to place something in rank order. For example, the respondent might be asked to place qualities or characteristics in order.

Scale
: There are various stages of scaling devices (nominal, ordinal, interval, ratio) which may be used in questionnaires, but they require careful handling.

Quantity
: The response is a number (exact or approximate), giving the amount of some characteristics.

Grid
: A table or grid is provided to record answers to two or more questions at the same time.

Students have discovered that once they have tried out and become familiar with different ways of analysing and presenting questionnaire responses to list, category, ranking, scale, quantity or grid questions, they are able to select the most appropriate format when they come to the stage of designing and analysing data in their project.

Question wording

Ambiguity, imprecision and assumption

Words which have a common meaning to you may mean something different to other people, so you need to consider what your questions might mean to different respondents. For example, suppose you want to find out how much time mature students spend studying. You ask:

How much time, on average, do you spend studying?	A great deal A certain amount Not much	☐ ☐ ☐

What will you do with the responses? What will they mean? 'A great deal' may mean something different for student A than for student B. In any case, students may spend twenty hours a week at some times of the year but probably not more than four at other times. What is 'average'? If you really wish to know how much time students spend studying, you will need to find different ways of putting the question. When you think about this topic you may decide you have to ask students to keep a diary for a specific period of time. You may need to specify the time spent studying different subjects. It will all depend on exactly what it is you need to know. Once you are clear about that, you will be able to word your questions sufficiently precisely to ensure that they mean the same to all respondents.

If respondents are confused, or if they hesitate over an answer, they may pass on to the next question. You want answers to all questions if at all possible, so try to avoid confusion.

The following question seems straightforward, but is it?

Which type of school does your child attend? (Please tick)	Infant school Primary school Comprehensive school Grammar school Other (please specify) ——————————— ———————————	☐ ☐ ☐ ☐ ☐

There is an assumption in this question that the respondent has one child. If she has none or four, one in an infant school, one in a primary school and two in a comprehensive school, what does she do? Does she tick all boxes or none? Does she put the number of children in the appropriate box? Are you prepared for a category response, or had you intended this to be a list? It may not matter, but if your analysis is planned on the basis of a category response, you will give yourself extra trouble when list responses are given. Incidentally, your respondents might well ask why you want this information. Do you? Is the information essential for your study? If not, leave it out.

Memory

Memory plays tricks. If you were asked to say which television programmes you saw last week, could you remember everything? Could you be sure that one particular programme was last week – or was it the week before? Consider the following question, which appeared in a questionnaire concerned with parents' education. At first sight, it seems pefectly clear.

What subjects did you study at school?

If respondents left school recently, they may be able to remember quite clearly, but if they left school 20 or more years ago, they may find it difficult to remember. If they do not include English in the list of subjects, would that mean that no English was studied or did they just forget to include it? Consider what information you really need. If you want to know which of a list of subjects that respondent studied, you might decide it would be better to provide a list of subjects which can be ticked. That way, you would ensure that main subjects were covered – but the type of question will depend on the type of information needed.

Knowledge

Take care over questions which ask for information that the respondents may not know or may not have readily to hand. For example, it may seem reasonable to ask mature students what the criteria are for allocating students to tutorial groups. But the likelihood is that they will not know: and if respondents have to search for information, they may decide to abandon the entire questionnaire.

Double questions

It may seem obvious to remind you that double questions should never be asked, but it is easy to overlook the following type of question:

Do you attend maths and chemistry classes?

Would the answer 'Yes' mean that you attend both, or one? If you need to know, the question should be divided into:

Do you attend maths classes?
and
Do you attend chemistry classes?

Leading questions

It is not always easy to spot a leading question, but the use of emotive language or the way a question is put can lead respondents to answer questions in one way. For example:

Do you not agree that mature students should have the right to express their views in tutorials?

Well, it might be difficult for students to answer 'No' in response to that question.

Presuming questions

Presuming questions are often a source of error in questionnaires. When they are included it is often because the researcher holds strong views about a subject and overlooks the fact that everyone may not feel the same way. For example:

Does the university/college make adequate provision for counselling?

You may think that all institutions should provide a counselling service. But what if your respondents do not? What if they do not really know what the counselling service does? In its present form, 'adequate' is meaningless. There is a presumption in the question that a counselling service is necessary, and that makes the question invalid.

Hypothetical questions

Watch for questions that will provide only useless responses. Most hypothetical questions come into this category. For example:

If you had no family responsibilities and plenty of money, what would you do with your life?

But, a respondent might answer, I do have family responsibilities. I have no money and never shall have as far as I can see, so what's the point of thinking about it?

Offensive questions and questions covering sensitive issues

It goes without saying that questions that may cause offence should be removed. If you really need information on what might be regarded by some respondents as sensitive issues, you will need to take extra care in the wording and positioning of questions. Some researchers think it is better to place such questions towards the end of the questionnaire, the theory being that if respondents abandon the questionnaire at that point, you at least have answers to all the earlier questions.

Age is often considered to be in the sensitive category and

rather than asking respondents to give their exact age, it may be better to ask them to indicate the category, as follows:

What is your age?
20 or younger ☐
21–24 ☐
25–29 ☐
30–34 ☐
35 or older ☐

Be careful not to have overlapping categories. It is not uncommon to see age categories listed as 21 or less, 21–25, 25–30, etc.

Appearance and layout

An excellently prepared questionnaire will lose much of its impact if it looks untidy. Look at some of the published surveys which used a questionnaire as one method of data collection and they will give you ideas about layout. Recipients need to be encouraged to read and to answer the questions and they may be put off by a scruffy document that has been hastily prepared. There are no hard-and-fast rules about layout, but there are a few common-sense guidelines that will help appearance.

1 Questionnaires should be typed (or printed, if you are conducting a very large survey).
2 Instructions should be clear (in capitals, or in a different font).
3 Spacing between questions will help the reader and will also help you when you analyse responses.
4 If you want to keep the questionnaire to a limited number of sheets, it may be better to photo-reduce copy.
5 Keep any response boxes in line towards the right of the sheet. This will make it easy for respondents and will help you to extract information.
6 If you intend to use a computer program, allow space on the right of the sheet for coding.
7 Look critically at your questionnaire and ask yourself what impression it would give if you were the recipient.
8 Take care over the order of the questions. Leave sensitive issues

to later in the questionnaire. Start with straightforward, easy-to-complete questions and move on to the more complex topics (writing questions on cards or separate pieces of paper will make it easy to sort and re-sort questions).

Drawing a sample

The number of subjects in your investigation will necessarily depend on the amount of time you have. If you are working on a 100-hour project, you will not be able to include all mature undergraduates in the country. If you have decided to restrict your research to one institution, then you will need to find out how many mature undergraduates are there. If there are 100 you will be unlikely to have the time or the means to include them all. You will need to select a sample.

In very large surveys, like the census, sampling techniques will be employed in order to produce a sample which is, as far as possible, representative of the population as a whole. Generalizations can then be made from the findings. In small studies, we have to do the best we can.

All researchers are dependent on the goodwill and availability of subjects, and it will probably be difficult for an individual researcher working on a small-scale project to achieve a true random sample. If that proves to be the case, you may be forced to interview anyone from the total population who is available and willing at the time. Opportunity samples of this kind are generally acceptable as long as the make-up of the sample is clearly stated and the limitations of such data are realized. However, even in a small study, efforts should be made to select as representative a sample as possible. Say you decide to include 50 per cent of your population. A random sample will give each of the individuals concerned an equal chance of being selected. You may decide to select alternate names on an alphabetical list, the first person being selected by sticking a pin in the paper. Everyone selected may not be willing to participate, and so it is wise to have reserve names available. For example, if the twentieth person refused or was not available, you might have decided beforehand, and as part of your research design, to approach the twenty-first.

There may be occasions when you wish to include representative sub-groups. You perhaps wish to select the appropriate proportion of men and women, of individuals in different age categories or some other sub-group of the target population. If so, you might have the following type of stratification.

Total target population: 100
Number of men: 60. Number of women: 40.

Instead of selecting alternate names, the sample population could be selected on the basis of every second man and every second woman, and so 30 men and 20 women would be selected.

If you wished to find out how many men and women had A levels on entry, you could take the process one step further, as follows:

	Men	Women	Total
Had A levels on entry	30	10	40
Did not have A levels on entry	30	30	60
Total	60	40	100

If sex and A levels on entry were particularly important, then the sub-groups would be specified as part of the research design, and the sample would be drawn in the appropriate proportion from each sub-group or cell. This is a rather crude example, but, for a small-scale exercise, it will generally be an acceptable way of selecting a sample. If a more scientific approach is required for your project, you will need to read further and to acquire a certain amount of statistical expertise.

Further reading is indicated at the end of the chapter.

Piloting the questionnaire

All data-gathering instruments should be piloted to test how long it takes recipients to complete them, to check that all questions and instructions are clear and to enable you to remove any items which do not yield usable data. There is a temptation in a small study to go straight to the distribution stage, but however pressed for time you are, do your best to give the questionnaire a trial run, even if you have to press-gang members of your family or friends. Ideally, it should be tried out on a group similar to the one that will form the population of your study, but if that is not possible, make do with whoever you can get. Respondents will tell you how long it took to complete the questionnaire, and if they leave any questions unanswered, you will be able to find out why. The purpose of a pilot exercise is to get the bugs out of the instrument so that subjects in your main study will experience no difficulties in completing it and so that you can carry out a preliminary analysis to see whether the wording and format of questions will present any difficulties when the main data are analysed.

Ask your guinea-pigs the following questions:

1 How long did it take you to complete?
2 Were the instructions clear?
3 Were any of the questions unclear or ambiguous? If so, will you say which and why?
4 Did you object to answering any of the questions?
5 In your opinion, has any major topic been omitted?
6 Was the layout of the questionnaire clear/attractive?
7 Any comments?

Their responses will enable you to revise the questionnaire ready for the main distribution. It will take you some time to achieve a good standard of design and presentation, but if the preparation is sound, it will save you hours and even weeks of work at the analysis stage.

Distribution and return of questionnaires

You will need to make an early decision about how to distribute your questionnaire and what to do about non-response. There are distinct advantages in being able to give questionnaires to subjects personally. You can explain the purpose of the study, and in some cases questionnaires can be completed on the spot. You are likely to get better cooperation if you can establish personal contact, but if that is impossible, you will need to investigate other ways of distribution. Permission can sometimes be obtained to distribute through internal mailing systems. Colleagues and friends may be persuaded to lend a hand. If all else fails, you may have to mail copies, but postal surveys are expensive and response rates are generally low, so you would only wish to resort to distribution by post if you found it impossible to contact subjects by any other means.

Unless you are meeting subjects face-to-face, an accompanying letter will be required, explaining the purpose of the questionnaire, indicating that official approval has been given (if that is the case) and saying what will be done with the information provided. Confidentiality and/or anonymity is usually promised, but before you promise either, decide what that means. Does it mean that there will be no way of identifying respondents or does it mean that only you and specified people will see the returns? Does it mean that you will publish the findings, but that no names will be mentioned in the report? Re-read Chapter 3 in which Stephen Waters talks about the problems he encountered over the principle of confidentiality and then decide what you can or cannot promise. It is important to be clear about this before questionnaires are distributed.

Take care with the wording of your letter. A letter that is too brusque or too ingratiating can have an adverse effect on response, so show your draft letter to a few friends and ask their opinion. Remember to give the return date, either in the letter or in a prominent position on the questionnaire. Experience has shown that it is unwise to allow too long. If no date is specified or if too long is given, it becomes too easy for subjects to put the questionnaire to one side, which often means that it will never be seen again. Two weeks is a reasonable time for completion. Give the precise day and date rather than relying on a polite request for the questionnaire to be returned in two weeks' time. For some reason, it seems to help to jog memories if the day as well as the date is stated.

Include a self-addressed envelope (stamped, if respondents have to return the questionnaire by post).

Non-response

Keep a careful record of the date questionnaires were distributed and the date they were returned. Generally, there is a good response at first and then returns slow down. Inevitably, all will not be returned by the specified date, so if you have decided to follow up non-respondents, a second letter and questionnaire will have to be sent.

If you do not ask for names to be given, or devise some system of numbering, you will have no way of knowing who has replied and who has not, and so there can be no follow up. If you promise anonymity, there can be no cunning little symbols that tell you who has replied. Anonymity means that there is no way of linking responses with individuals, so a decision has to be made about follow up *before* the questionnaires are distributed. As Moser and Kalton (1971: 267–8) point out, 'non-response is a problem because of the likelihood – repeatedly confirmed in practice – that people who do not return questionnaires differ from those who do'! Scott (1961), whose article 'Research on mail surveys' is a major resource for investigators undertaking large-scale projects involving postal questionnaires, takes the view that if non-response is as low as 10 per cent, in most cases it does not matter very much how biased the non-respondents are, but a higher non-response rate could distort results, and so, if at all possible, some effort should be made to encourage more people to return completed questionnaires.

Opinions vary as to the best time to send out follow-up requests, but in a limited-time project you will need to write about a week after the original date if you are to complete data collection in the time allocated. In some large projects a third and even a fourth reminder will be sent, but the number of returns obtained by this process is unlikely to warrant the time and trouble it will involve.

Analysis of data

In an ideal world it would be best to wait for all questionnaires to be returned and to glance through all responses before beginning to code and record. In a limited-time project it may be necessary to begin recording responses as soon as the first questionnaires are returned. The procedures for analysing and presenting results, described in Chapter 12, may influence the way you structure the questionnaire and word the questions, so before you decide finally on content and format, read this chapter carefully.

⊙ Questionnaire checklist

1	Decide what you need to know.	List all items about which information is required.
2	Ask yourself why you need this information.	Examine your list and remove any item that is not directly associated with the task.
3	Is a questionnaire the best way of obtaining the information?	Consider alternatives.
4	If so, begin to word questions.	Write questions on separate cards or pieces of paper, to help ordering later on. Consider question type (verbal, grid, etc.).
5	Check wording of each question. Is there any ambiguity, imprecision or assumption? Are you asking respondents to remember? Will they be able to? Are you asking for knowledge respondents may not have? Any double, leading, presuming, hypothetical or offensive questions?	Keep language simple. Don't use words respondents may not understand (that includes technical language), unless you are dealing with a professional group all of whom understand your linguistic short cuts.
6	Decide on the question type.	Verbal, list, category, ranking, scale, quantity or grid. Each type requires a different analysis (see Chapter 12 for further information).
7	When you are satisfied that all questions are well worded and of the right type, sort into order.	It is often best to leave sensitive issues until later in the questionnaire.

8 Write out instructions to be included on the questionnaire.	Respondents must be quite clear about how they are to answer questions (ticks in boxes, Yes/No, etc.).
9 Consider layout and appearance.	Instructions must be clearly presented (perhaps different font displayed in a prominent position?) Decide whether you need a right-hand margin for coding.
10 Hand over your questionnaire for typing or printing – or type it yourself.	Instructions to the typist must be absolutely clear. It is your job to decide how the questionnaire should be displayed, not the typist's.
11 Decide on your sample.	If possible, select a sample which will give you subjects who are likely to be representative of the population. If you have to make do with an opportunity sample, say why in your report.
12 Pilot your questionnaire.	Ideally, it should be sent to people who are similar to your selected sample. However, if that is not possible, ask friends, family or colleagues to help.
13 Try out your methods of analysis. **Read Chapter 12 before you decide finally on format and analysis.**	Even with five or six completed questionnaires, you will be able to see whether any problems are likely to arise when you analyse the main returns.
14 Make any adjustments to the questionnaire in the light of pilot respondents' comments and your preliminary analysis.	Consider timing. It if took your guinea-pigs too long to complete, consider whether any items might be removed.
15 Decide at an early stage how the questionnaires are to be distributed.	By post? Internal mail? By you? If you decide on a postal survey, include a stamped addressed envelope. People are doing you a favour by completing the

	questionnaire. Don't expect them to pay for the privilege.
16 Unless you are administering the questionnaire personally, include a covering letter and a self-addressed envelope.	Explain the purpose of the study. If you have official approval to carry out the study, say so.
17 Don't forget to say when you would like questionnaires to be returned.	Keep a record of when questionnaires were distributed and when returned.
18 Decide what you are going to do about non-respondents BEFORE you distribute the questionnaires.	Remember you will not be able to send out reminders if all responses are anonymous.
19 Do not distribute questionnaires before checking whether approval is required.	Never assume 'it will be all right'.
20 Begin to record data as soon as completed questionnaires are returned.	You have no time to wait for stragglers.
21 Do not get involved with complicated statistics unless you know what you are doing.	It is perfectly possible to produce a good report without extensive statistical knowledge, as long as the structure of the questionnaire is well thought out.

Further reading

Most books dealing with research methods will have a chapter on the design of questionnaires and so the only items listed here are standard texts which should be readily available in libraries. All provide good advice and will provide a sound foundation if you plan to design a questionnaire as part of your investigation.

Moser, C.A. and Kalton, G. (1971) *Survey Methods in Social Investigation*. London: Heinemann. See Chapters 11 and 13.

Oppenheim, A.N. (1966) *Questionnaire Design and Attitude Measurement*. London, Heinemann. Rather old now, but still provides a wealth of information about questionnaire design.

Scott, C. (1961) 'Research on mail surveys', *Journal of the Royal Statistical Society*, Series A (124), 143–205. This article is well worth study, if it can be obtained. If not, many of the issues Scott discusses are covered in Moser and Kalton.

Youngman, M.B. (1982) *Designing and Analysing Questionnaires*. Rediguide 12. University of Nottingham, School of Education. Also reproduced as Chapter 10 in Bell, J. *et al.* (1984) *Conducting Small-scale Investigations in Educational Management*. London: Harper & Row. One of the best and most straightforward guides to questionnaire design and distribution. A revised version of this Rediguide appears as Chapter 17 in Bennett *et al.* (1994) *Improving Educational Management through Research and Consultancy*. London: Paul Chapman.

9

PLANNING AND CONDUCTING INTERVIEWS

A major advantage of the interview is its adaptability. A skilful interviewer can follow up ideas, probe responses and investigate motives and feelings, which the questionnaire can never do. The way in which a response is made (the tone of voice, facial expression, hesitation, etc.) can provide information that a written response would conceal. Questionnaire responses have to be taken at face value, but a response in an interview can be developed and clarified.

There are problems of course. Interviews are time-consuming, and so in a 100-hour project you will be able to interview only a relatively small number of people. It is a highly subjective technique and therefore there is always the danger of bias. Analysing responses can present problems, and wording the questions is almost as demanding for interviews as it is for questionnaires. Even so, the interview can yield rich material and can often put flesh on the bones of questionnaire responses.

Moser and Kalton (1971: 271) describe the survey interview as 'a conversation between interviewer and respondent with the purpose of eliciting certain information from the respondent'. This, they continue, might appear a straightforward matter, but the attainment of a successful interview is much more complex than this statement might suggest.

Wiseman and Aron (1972) liken interviewing to a fishing

expedition and, pursuing this analogy, Cohen (1976: 82) adds that 'like fishing, interviewing is an activity requiring careful preparation, much patience, and considerable practice if the eventual reward is to be a worthwhile catch'.

Preparation for interviews follows much the same procedures as for questionnaires. Topics need to be selected, questions devised, methods of analysis considered, a schedule prepared and piloted.

Though question wording is important, it may not be quite as important to be precise about the use of certain terms as for questionnaires, though of course the language you use must be understandable to the respondents. In the chapter on questionnaire design, I gave the example of students having been asked how much time they spent studying and suggested that 'a great deal', 'a certain amount' and 'not much', would mean different things to different people. In an interview, it would be possible to ask 'How much time do you spend studying?' and then to follow with a prompt on the lines of 'For example . . .'

Follow the rules laid down for questionnaire design (no leading, presumptive or offensive questions, etc.). Prepare topics and then questions on cards or on separate pieces of paper, so that you can decide the order of questioning when all topics have been covered. Consider which is likely to be the best order in which to ask questions. The order may be important in establishing an easy relationship with the interviewee. The manner in which you ask questions most certainly will be. Practise interviewing and managing your schedule to make sure your form of questioning is clear, does not antagonize the respondent and allows you to record responses in a way that you can understand when the interview is over.

Type of interview

Once you have decided what you need to know, a decision will have to be made about the type of interview which is most likely to produce the information required. Grebenik and Moser (1962: 16) see the alternative types as ranged somewhere on what they call 'a continuum of formality'. At one extreme is the completely formalized interview where the interviewer behaves as much like a machine as possible. At the other is the completely informal interview in which the shape is determined by individual respondents. The more standardized the interview, the easier it is to aggregate and quantify the results. A structured interview can take the form of a questionnaire or checklist that is completed by the interviewer rather than by the respondent, and if you are a first-time interviewer, you may find it easier to use a structured format.

In the case of your investigation into barriers to learning, you might perhaps wish to find out the extent to which mature students have participated in the activities of the Mature Students' Society. In that case, you might prepare a schedule on the following lines:

Date of interview:		Name of interviewee:		
Venue:		Department:		
Topic:	Mature Students' Society participation			
	To what extent have you participated in the activities of the Mature Students' Society?			
Prompt	Social events?	1	2	3
	Representation on university committees?	1	2	3
	Peer support groups?	1	2	3
	Anything else?			
1 = not at all;				
2 = to a certain extent (ask for examples)				
3 = a great deal (ask for examples)				

If the interviewee provides information freely, then prompts will not be necessary, but if you particularly wish to know, for example, whether students made use of peer support groups and whether they found them useful, then a prompt may be needed.

The above format allows you to circle responses and if plenty of space is allowed, any interesting comments provided by the interviewee can be jotted down. It saves a great deal of time at the analysis stage and you can be sure all topics are covered. The problem about this format is that you, as the interviewer, decide what questions to ask – and you may not be asking the important questions.

Unstructured interviews centred round a topic may, and in skilled hands do, produce a wealth of valuable data, but such interviews require a great deal of expertise to control and a great deal of time to analyse. Conversation about a topic may be interesting and may produce useful insights into a problem, but it has to be remembered that an interview is more than just an interesting conversation. You need certain information and methods have to be devised to obtain that information if at all possible.

Preliminary interviews can probably be placed at the 'completely unstructured' end of the continuum of formality. This is the stage when you are trying to find out which areas or topics are important and when people directly concerned with the topic are encouraged to talk about what is of central significance to them. At this stage you are looking for clues as to which areas should be explored and which left out. Interviews of this kind require only the minimum of note-taking, and as long as your notes are clear enough to enable you to extract points of interest, and topics for inclusion in the study, they will suffice.

Most interviews carried out in the main data-collecting stage of the research will come somewhere between the completely structured and the completely unstructured point on the continuum. Freedom to allow the respondent to talk about what is of central significance to him or her rather than to the interviewer is clearly important, but some loose structure to ensure all topics which are considered crucial to the study are covered does eliminate some of the problems of entirely unstructured interviews. The guided or focused interview fulfils these requirements. No questionnaire or checklist is used, but a framework is established by selecting topics around which the interview is guided. The respondent is allowed a considerable degree of latitude within the framework. Certain questions are asked, but respondents are given freedom to talk about the topic and give their views in their own time. The interviewer needs to have the skill to ask questions and, if necessary, to probe at the right time, but if the interviewee moves freely from one topic to another, the conversation can flow without interruption.

The advantage of a focused interview is that a framework is established beforehand and so analysis is greatly simplified. This is important for any research, but particularly so for limited-time studies.

The type of interview selected will to an extent depend on the nature of the topic and what exactly you wish to find out. Preliminary interviews are held to give you ideas about which topics to include in the study, and so an unstructured approach is needed. Where specific information is required, it is generally wise to establish some sort of structure or you may end with a huge amount of information, no time to exploit it and still without the information you need.

Bias

There is always the danger of bias creeping into interviews, largely because, as Selltiz *et al.* (1962: 583) point out, 'interviewers are human beings and not machines', and their manner may have an effect on the respondents. Where a team of interviewers is employed, serious bias may show up in data analysis, but if one researcher conducts a set of interviews, the bias may be consistent and therefore go unnoticed.

Many factors can influence responses, one way or another. Borg draws attention to a few of the problems that may occur:

> Eagerness of the respondent to please the interviewer, a vague antagonism that sometimes arises between interviewer and respondent, or the tendency of the interviewer to seek out the answers that support his preconceived notions are but few of the factors that may contribute to biasing of data obtained from the interview. These factors are called *response effect* by survey researchers.
>
> (Borg 1981: 87)

It is easier to acknowledge the fact that bias can creep in than to eliminate it altogether. Gavron, who carried out research into the position and opportunities of young mothers, was very conscious of the dangers inherent in research by solitary interviewers. She wrote, 'It is difficult to see how this [i.e. bias] can be avoided completely, but awareness of the problem plus constant self-control can help' (Gavron 1966: 159).

If you know you hold strong views about some aspect of the

topic, you need to be particularly careful about the way questions are put. It is even easier to 'lead' in an interview than it is in a questionnaire. The same question put by two people, but with different emphasis and in a different tone of voice can produce very different responses. Complete objectivity is the aim.

Recording and verification

If you are using a structured format which enables you to tick or circle a previously prepared questionnaire or checklist, you should leave the interview with a set of responses that can be easily analysed. If you are using a less-structured approach, you will need to devise some means of recording responses. Some researchers tape-record interviews (with the respondent's permission) and, if they have ample secretarial support, analyse responses from the transcript. You are unlikely to have such support readily available, and if you have to transcribe yourself, you will have to find something in the region of ten hours for each hour recorded. It is questionable whether you can afford so much time and whether the outcome will be worth the effort. Tape recordings can be useful to check the wording of any statement you might wish to quote and to check that your notes are accurate. They can also be useful if you are attempting some form of content analysis and need to be able to listen several times in order to identify categories. However, with experience, interviewers learn to devise shorthand systems of their own, and as long as notes can be written up immediately, or very soon after the interview ends, it is possible to produce a reasonable record of what was said in the key areas. Careful preparation of an interview guide or schedule will help you to record responses under prepared headings. Prompts listed on the schedule may never be used as prompts, but will serve as subheadings and will provide some structure for your note-taking.

Whenever possible, interview transcripts, and particularly statements that will be used as direct quotations in the report, should be verified with the respondent. The last thing you want is for a statement to be challenged at the report stage. However, remember some of the difficulties and time constraints Stephen Waters faced (Chapter 3). Just do your best in the time at your disposal.

Time, place and style of the interview

People who agree to be interviewed deserve some consideration and so you will need to fit in with their plans, however inconvenient it may be for you. Try to fix a venue and a time when you will not be disturbed. Trying to interview when a telephone is constantly ringing and people are knocking at the door will destroy any chance of continuity.

Before you begin to make appointments, make sure official channels, if any, have been cleared. A letter from your supervisor, your head or principal, saying what you are doing and why will always help.

It is difficult to lay down rules for the conduct of an interview. Common sense and normal good manners will, as always, take you a long way, but there are one or two courtesies that should always be observed. If your organization requires you to conform to an ethics protocol, or if you plan to use conditions and guarantees of your own, do your best to ensure your interviewee has sight of them beforehand. You should always introduce yourself and explain the purpose of the research, even if you have an official introductory letter. Make it quite clear what you will do with the information and check whether quotations and views must be anonymous or whether they can be attributed. When you make the appointment, say how long the interview is likely to last and do your best not to exceed the stated time. It is very easy to become so interested in the topic of discussion that time slips by and before you know it, you have exceeded the time limit.

Johnson (1984) makes the point that it is the responsibility of the interviewer, not the interviewee to end an interview. She writes:

It may have been difficult to negotiate access and to get in in the first place, but the interviewer who, once in, stays until he is thrown out, is working in the style of investigative journalism rather than social research . . . If an interview takes two or three times as long as the interviewer said it would, the respondent, whose other work or social activities have been accordingly delayed, will be irritated in retrospect, however enjoyable the experience may have been at the time. This sort of practice breaks one of the ethics of professional social research, which is that the field should not be left more difficult for subsequent investigators to explore by disenchanting respondents with the whole notion of research participation.

(Johnson 1984: 14–15)

Interviewing is not easy and many researchers have found it difficult to strike the balance between complete objectivity and trying to put the interviewee at ease. There are particular difficulties in interviewing senior colleagues, as Stephen Waters found when he interviewed his headmaster. He wrote as follows:

When interviewing members of the senior staff in the school and, in particular, the headmaster, I was conscious of the degree to which my status as a teacher placed me in a subordinate position, while paradoxically my role as researcher gave me the kind of advantage which Platt (1981) reports is inherent in the interviewer–interviewee relationship. I never managed to relieve the feeling of discomfort which arose from tying to reconcile the two roles. I am certain that the headmaster must have felt a similar internal conflict. It could not have been easy to discuss the school's management process with an inexperienced researcher who was also a member of his own staff. It is to the credit of all the participants that I did not, as far as I can tell, experience anything other than openness and honesty and thereby overcame what might have been a serious limitation to my inside research. Naturally, respondents chose their words carefully as they were aware that colleagues were to be given the opportunity of reading the final report. Diplomacy rather than concealment seemed to be their overriding consideration.

It is difficult to know how these difficulties can be overcome. Honesty about the purpose of the exercise, integrity in the conduct and in the reporting of the interview and a promise to allow interviewees to see the transcript and/or the draft of the report if possible, will all help, though cost and time may make it difficult to circulate drafts. Whatever promises are made must be kept, so take care not to promise too much.

A few words of warning

Interviews are very time-consuming. If you allow one hour for the actual interview, there is also travelling time and time lost through any one of numerous mishaps (respondent late home, sudden crisis with children which causes delay, unexpected visitor who interrupts the interview, etc.). Then there is the time needed to consider what has been said during the interview, to go through notes, to extend and clarify points that may have been hastily noted. If you are working full-time, you are unlikely to be able to carry out more than one interview in an evening, and even if you are able to devote yourself full-time to the task, it is difficult to cope with more than three or four interviews during the course of a day. Your original project plan should take account of the time required for planning and conducting interviews, for coping with cancelled arrangements, second visits and finding replacements for people who drop out.

⦿ Interview checklist

1 Decide what you need to know.	List all the items about which information is required.
2 Ask yourself why you need this information.	Examine your list and remove any item that is not directly associated with the task.
3 Is an interview the best way of obtaining the information?	Consider alternatives.
4 If so, begin to devise questions in outline.	The final form of questions will depend on the type of interview (and vice versa).
5 Decide the type of interview.	A structured interview will produce structured responses. Is this what you want, or is a more open approach required?
6 Refine the questions.	Write questions on cards. Check wording (see questionnaire checklist).
7 Consider how questions will be analysed.	Consult Chapter 12 before deciding finally about question type.

8 Prepare an interview schedule or guide.	Consider the order of questions. Prepare prompts in case the respondent does not provide essential information freely.
9 Pilot your schedule.	Schedules need to be tested, and you need practice in asking questions and recording responses.
10 Revise the schedule, if necessary.	Take account of pilot respondents' comments.
11 Do your best to avoid bias.	If you have strong views about some aspect of the topic, be particularly vigilant. If someone else asked the same question, would they get the same answer?
12 Select who to interview.	Interviews take time. Try to select a representative sample. Decide what to do if selected people are not willing or able to give an interview. Be realistic about the number of interviews that can be conducted in the time available.
13 Try to fix a time and place in which you will not be disturbed.	
14 Make sure official channels have been cleared, and let interviewees see any protocol documents beforehand.	A letter from your supervisor, head or principal, explaining the purpose of the research will be helpful.
15 Introduce yourself, explain the purpose of the research, even if you have a letter.	Say what you intend to do with the information the interviewee gives. Agree anonymity or whether statements can be attributed (see Chapter 3).
16 Say how long the interview will last.	Do your utmost not to exceed the time limit.
17 Try to check the accuracy of your notes with respondents (particularly	This will take time. Remember to allow for it in your planning. Don't promise to check with

items to be quoted in the report).	respondents if this is likely to prove difficult.
18 Decide whether to tape-record the interview.	Remember it will take a long time to transcribe. Permission must be given. Remember also that if an interview is recorded, it may affect the way a respondent words answers.
19 Honesty and integrity are important.	Make no promises that cannot be fulfilled. Respect respondents' views about anonymity. If you know a respondent has been indiscreet in revealing confidential information, never take advantage.
20 Common sense and good manners will take you a long way.	People who agree to be interviewed are doing you a favour. They deserve some consideration.
21 Don't queer the pitch for other researchers by disenchanting respondents with the whole notion of research participation.	There are any number of ways in which participants can become disenchanted. Appointments not kept or the interviewer arriving late; taking longer than promised; promising to check for accuracy and not doing so; conducting the interview in a hostile manner; failing to thank the respondent.

Further reading

As in the case of questionnaires, most standard books on research methods will have chapters relating to interviewing. Some of the best known are as follows:

Brenner, M., Brown, J. and Canter, D. (1985) *The Research Interview: Uses and Approaches*. New York: Academic Press. This is a collection of readings which cover many of the problems as well as the advantages of interviewing in social research. Quite a hard read at times.

Burgess, R.G. (1982) 'The unstructured interview as conversation' in Burgess, R.G. (ed.) *Field Research: A Source Book and Field Manual.* London: Allen & Unwin.

Cohen, L. and Manion, L. (1994) 'The interview', Chapter 13 in *Research Methods in Education*, 4th edn. London: Routledge.

Fidler, B. (1992) 'Telephone interviewing' reprinted as Chapter 19 in Bennett, N. *et al.* (1994) *Improving Educational Management through Research and Consultancy.* London: Paul Chapman.

May, T. (1993) 'Interviewing: methods and process', Chapter 6 in *Social Research Issues, Methods and Process.* Buckingham: Open University Press.

Moser, C.A. and Kalton, G. (1971) 'Methods of collecting the information III – Interviewing', Chapter 12 in *Survey Methods in Social Investigation.* London: Heinemann.

Powney, J. and Watts, M. (1987) *Interviewing in Educational Research.* London: Routledge & Kegan Paul.

Wragg, E.C. (1980) *Conducting and Analysing Interviews.* Rediguide 11, University of Nottingham, School of Education. Also reproduced as Chapter 11 in Bell, J. *et al.* (1984) *Conducting Small-scale Investigations in Educational Management.* London: Harper & Row, and as Chapter 18 in Bennett *et al.* (1994) *Improving Educational Management through Research and Consultancy.* London: Paul Chapman.

10

DIARIES

On the face of it, diaries are an attractive way of gathering information about the way individuals spend their time. Such diaries are not records of engagements or personal journals of thoughts and activities, but records or logs of professional activities. They can provide valuable information about work patterns and activities, provided subjects are clear what they are being asked to do, and why. Completing diary forms is time-consuming, and can be irritating for a busy person who has to keep stopping work to make an entry. If subjects are not fully in sympathy with the task, or have been press-ganged into filling in diary forms, they will probably not complete them thoroughly, if at all. As in all research activities it is essential to meet the people who will be giving up their time, so that you can explain the purpose of the excercise fully, inquire about likely problems and, if possible, resolve them. Reluctant subjects will rarely provide usable data, so preliminary consultation is of the utmost importance.

Oppenheim draws attention to a major problem with this technique:

> that the respondent's interest in filling up the diary will cause him to modify the very behaviour we wish him to record. If, for instance, he is completing a week's diary of his television-viewing behavior, this may cause him to engage in 'duty

viewing' in order to 'have something to record', or he may view 'better' types of programs in order to create a more favorable impression.

(Oppenheim 1966: 215)

Diaries generally cover an agreed time-span – a day, a week, a month, or occasionally much longer – depending on what information is required. At certain specified times, 'on the spot' or retrospectively, subjects are asked to say what they did. Diaries deal mainly with behaviour rather than emotions, though they can be adapted to suit whatever purpose you have in mind. Requests for information often take the form of:

'How often in the last hour (day, week, etc.) have you . . .?'
'In the past seven days have you done one of the following? (a), (b), (c), etc.'
'Write down all the things that you did between 4 and 5 o'clock in the afternoon.'

Instructions need to be explicit. Do you really want to know that someone had a cup of tea, paid the milkman or had a bath, or are you only interested in specifically job-related activities?

In any diary exercise there are problems with representativeness. Was this day of the week typical of others or is Monday always the crisis day? Is this week exceptional? As with any other form of data-collecting, some form of check is often desirable.

The diary–interview method

As Burgess (1981) notes, diaries can be used as a preliminary to interviewing. Zimmerman and Wieder used them in this way for their ethnographic study of the counter-culture in the USA. In an article on the diary interview method they describe the purpose of diaries:

Individuals are commissioned by the investigator to maintain . . . a record over some specified period of time according to a set of instructions. The employment of diary materials in this

sense, when coupled with an interview (or series of interviews) based on the diary, is also similar to the 'life-history'
method . . . The technique we describe emphasizes the role of
diaries as an observational log maintained by subjects which
can then be used as a basis for intensive interviewing.

(Zimmerman and Wieder 1977: 481)

So Zimmerman and Wieder see a use for diaries as a preliminary
for interviewing in cases where it may not at first be clear what are
the right questions to ask, and

the diarist's statement is used as a way of generating questions
for the subsequent diary interview. The diary interview con-
verts the diary – a source of data in its own right – into a question-generating and, hence, data-generating device.

(p. 489)

The potential for diaries as question-generating devices is clear,
but Zimmerman and Wieder take this process a step further. They
view the use of a diary, in conjunction with the diary interview, as
an approximation to the method of participant observation. They
point to some of the difficulties of participant observation,
including: the length of time involved; the fact that any observer,
even a participant, may have an effect on normal behaviour; and,
in some studies, moral, legal or ethical constraints. They propose
the use of the diary interview method 'for those situations where
the problems of direct observation resist solution, or where
further or more extended observation strains available resources'
(p. 481).

They asked their subjects to record in chronological order the
activities in which they engaged over a seven-day period, following the formula what/when/where/how?

The 'What?' involved a description of the activity or discussion recorded in the diarists' own categories. 'When?' involved reference to the time and timing of the activity, with
special attention to recording the actual sequence of events.
'Where?' involved a designation of the location of the activity,
suitably coded to prevent identification of individuals or

places. The 'How?' involved a description of whatever logistics
were entailed by the activity.

(p. 486)

Clearly, diarists must be of a certain educational level to understand the instructions, let alone complete the diary. They must
also have time. If you are asking colleagues to cooperate by completing diaries, be very sure that the diary is the best way of
obtaining the information you need and that you can convince
your subjects that what they are doing is likely to be of practical
use.

A less wide-ranging approach was adopted by Bradley and
Eggleston (1976) in their study of probationer teachers in three
LEAs. Probationer teachers were asked to keep weekly diaries on
three separate occasions during the term. This asked for information about professional activities in which teachers might have
engaged, outside scheduled teaching time. A form was provided
for each day of the week, including the weekend.

In addition to keeping the weekly diaries, the probationer
teachers were asked to make a note of things to which they gave
a lot of thought during the day (e.g. problems of non-readers,
keeping noise to an acceptable level), to make a list of people with
whom they had discussed matters relating to their work and to
indicate what they had done in any periods when they were
released from teaching.

The types of question will, of course, reflect the emphasis of the
study. Completed diaries can provide a wealth of information,
and this can be a problem in itself unless the same care is taken
in wording the questions as is necessary for questionnaires and
interviews, and unless thought has been given as to how the
information will be analysed, *before* the diaries are designed
and completed.

Holly (1984: 5) adds her own concerns about the difficulties of
handling the data:

> Because diary writing is interpretive, descriptive, on multiple
> dimensions, unstructured, sometimes factual and often all
> of these, it is difficult to analyse. It is not easy to separate
> thoughts from feelings from facts . . .

It is as well to take account of such difficulties, though that is not to say that attempts to find out how individuals spend their time should be abandoned. If difficulties over the management of diaries prove to be insurmountable, then it is a case of identifying alternative approaches. Oxtoby (1979: 239–40) suggests that in some circumstances the identification of 'critical incidents' and the production of 'problem portfolios' may produce more worthwhile data.

The critical-incidents and problem-portfolio approaches

One way of investigating the work people do is to ask them to describe what 'critical incidents' occurred over a specified period of time (Flanagan 1951, 1954). Writing about the problems facing heads of department in further education, Oxtoby asks how heads of department can attempt to find out how their time is spent, and how they can sift the key aspects of their job from the trivial ones:

> Analysing work activities can be approached from many different points of view . . . Some methods are not capable of being used by HoDs to monitor their own activities, for example, interviews, observation and activity sampling, questionnaires and checklists. More appropriate methods are those which rely on written activity records of one kind or another, such as diaries, critical incident reports, problem portfolios. The use of a job diary is perhaps the most simple and widely accepted way of finding out how time is spent. But self-recording can be inaccurate – many of the shorter episodes tend to get omitted – and compiling a detailed diary is usually a tiresome and onerous business. Although it is undoubtedly valuable in terms of enabling people to make more effective use of their time, a diary does not provide much reliable information about the skills or qualities developed. Moreover, the prospect of using diaries to compare differences between large numbers of staff and their jobs is extremely daunting, if only because of the difficulties involved in handling the data. There are snags, therefore, in

employing job diaries to analyse the diversity of HoD activities.

The critical incident technique is an attempt to identify the more 'noteworthy' aspects of job behaviour and is based on the assumption that jobs are composed of critical and non-critical tasks. For example, a critical task might be defined as one which makes the difference between success and failure in carrying out important parts of the job. The idea is to collect reports as to what people do that is particularly effective in contributing to good performance and then to scale the incidents in order of difficulty, frequency and importance to the job as a whole. The technique scores over the use of diaries in that it is centred on specific happenings and on what is judged to be effective behaviour. But it is still laborious and does not lend itself to objective quantification.

(Oxtoby 1979: 239–40)

Oxtoby concluded that a more flexible and productive approach to his particular task of identifying the problems faced by heads of department in colleges would be to adopt the methods advocated by Marples (1967)

who suggests that one measure of a manager's ability may be expressed in terms of the number and duration of 'issues' or *problems* being tackled at any one time. He advocates the compilation of 'problem portfolios', recording information about how each problem arose, methods used to solve it, difficulties encountered and so on. Such an analysis also raises questions about the job incumbent's use of time: what proportion of his time is occupied in checking; in handling problems given to him by others; on self-generated problems; on 'top priority' problems; on minor issues?

(Oxtoby 1979: 240)

In his study, Oxtoby sent a questionnaire to 240 heads of department in colleges of further education in England and Wales, asking them 'What was the most difficult task or situation with which you had to deal during the past two or three days?' Another way of approaching the task would have been to ask heads of department to complete a diary over a period of one week, asking them to describe in about ten lines the most difficult problem or situation they had to deal with each day, why it arose, why it was difficult and how they acted.

In a 100-hour project, you are unlikely to survey 240 departments, but you may wish to ask mature undergraduates how much time they spend studying and which subjects make the greatest demands on their time. If so, critical-incidents or problem-portfolio techniques may be appropriate. They have the advantage of not requiring your subjects to spend substantial amounts of time completing a diary with what may seem rather trivial items, and they allow you to see what the subjects themselves considered to be problems.

As will be apparent from the above, there are problems in the use of diaries as a method of gathering evidence, not least the time needed to complete the forms. However, diaries can produce a wealth of interesting data and are relatively simple to administer. Analysis of completed forms is not so simple however, so you will need to consider how responses will be coded before you put your subjects to the trouble of filling in the diaries. If you are using diaries as part of a project, you may wish to consult the checklist at the end of this chapter before you distribute them.

One final point about the use of diaries as research tools. Burgess (1994: 310) reminds us that there are ethical issues surrounding the use of diaries and diary keeping, particularly as they relate to intrusion:

> In many instances, diaries are advocated as a means of gaining access to situations in which it would not normally be possible to obtain data. However, it could be argued that the researcher intrudes further into the lives and work of teachers and pupils in a far greater way than when observations are made in schools and classrooms. Here, the trade-off has to be considered between the information required and the degree of intrusion into the lives of individuals.

As always, permission will need to be obtained *and* full and complete information provided about what is required, in what form and for what purpose. If that is done, and your own code of practice is followed, all should be well.

⊙ Diaries and critical-incidents checklist

1 Decide what you need to know.

List all the items about which information is required.

2 Ask yourself why you need this information.

You may decide you don't need it after all.

3 Is a diary or critical-incidents checklist the best way of obtaining the information?

Would another approach be better?

4 Diary completion is not generally a suitable tool for use with people of limited educational background.

Make sure your subjects will be able to fulfil the requirements.

5 Instructions must be precise.

Subjects must be quite clear what it is you want them to do and when.

6 Make sure subjects know *why* they are being asked to carry out this chore and what you plan to do with the information.

Allow time at the planning stage to discuss with your subjects what is involved.

7 Decide how to propose to deal with responses *before* you ask for diaries to be completed.

8 Try to find time to check progress.

If you are asking people to carry out this task for more than one day, evidence seems to indicate that a solicitous inquiry about how things are going may help them to keep on with the task.

9 Remember to get permission to approach subjects.

Never assume 'it will be all right'.

10 Completing a diary is a chore. Don't forget to thank your subjects.

Give them feedback if you can, but don't promise anything if you are unlikely to have the time.

Further reading

Bogdan, R. and Taylor, S.J. (1975) *Introduction to Qualitative Research Methods*. London, Wiley. Provides examples of ways in which diagrams can be used in research diaries.

Burgess, R.G. (1981) 'Keeping a research diary', *Cambridge Journal of Education*, 11, Part 1, 75–83. Also reproduced as Chapter 12 in Bell, J. *et al.* (1984) *Conducting Small-scale Investigations in Educational Management*. London: Harper & Row.

Burgess, R.G. (1982) *Field Research: A Source Book and Field Manual*. London: Allen & Unwin.

Burgess, R.G. (1994) 'On diaries and diary keeping', Chapter 21 in Bennett *et al. Improving Educational Management through Research and Consultancy*. London: Paul Chapman.

Oppenheim, A.N. (1966) *Introduction to Qualitative Research Methods*. London: Wiley. Provides examples of ways in which diagrams can be used in research diaries.

11

OBSERVATION STUDIES

The teacher researcher, or the student working on his own, is at no disadvantage compared to the research team when he is working personally on observation and analysis of individual instances. Observation, however, is not a 'natural' gift but a highly skilled activity for which an extensive background knowledge and understanding is required, and also a capacity for original thinking and the ability to spot significant events. It is certainly not an easy option.

(Nisbet 1977: 15)

Anyone who has carried out an observation study will no doubt agree with Nisbet that observation is not an easy option. Careful planning and piloting are essential, and it takes practice to get the most out of this technique. However, once mastered, it is a technique that can often reveal characteristics of groups or individuals which would have been impossible to discover by other means. Interviews, as Nisbet and Watt (1980: 13) point out, provide important data, but they reveal only how people *perceive* what happens, not what actually happens. Direct observation may be more reliable than what people say in many instances. It can be particularly useful to discover whether people do what they say they do, or behave in the way they claim to behave.

There are two main types of observation – *participant* and

non-participant. Lacy (1976: 65) defined a participant observation as 'the transfer of the whole person into an imaginative and emotional experience in which the fieldworker learned to live in and understand the new world'. He was writing about his experiences at 'Hightown Grammar' where, for three years, he taught, observed classes and talked to teachers and pupils. He describes his methodology in *The Organisation and Impact of Social Research.*

There are numbers of other well-documented examples of researchers spending months or years in a community in order to become immersed in its life so that they are generally accepted as one of the group. Most studies of this kind are largely unstructured. That is, the researchers do not start with preconceived ideas about precisely what it is they want to observe. They have no checklists or charts. They observe events, situations, behaviour and then write up all their observations immediately afterwards. Lacey could not do his job as a teacher and at the same time carry around checklists and charts.

There are problems with this approach, not least the researcher's interpretation of what is seen. If three or four people stand at a window overlooking a busy street, observing what is going on for five minutes or so, and then write up what they have seen, the accounts are likely to vary. The observers will have their own particular focus and interpret significant events in their own way.

Unstructured observation can be useful to generate hypotheses, but it is time-consuming and it is not easy to manage. Methods of cross-checking have to be introduced. Field notes which are written up as soon as possible after the observation take time, and interpretation of the notes requires experience – and even more time.

Cohen and Manion (1994: 110–11) draw attention to some of the criticisms levelled at participant observation:

> The accounts that typically emerge from participant observation are often described as subjective, biased, impressionistic, idiosyncratic and lacking in the precise quantifiable measures that are the hallmark of survey research and experimentation. While it is probably true that nothing can give better insight into the life of a gang of juvenile delinquents

than going to live with them for an extended period of time, critics of participant observation will point to the dangers of 'going native' as a result of playing a role within such a group.

Participant observers are well aware of the dangers of bias. It is difficult to stand back and adopt the role of objective observer when all the members of the group or organization are known to you. If you are researching in your own organization, you will be familiar with the personalities, strengths and weaknesses of colleagues, and this familiarity may cause you to overlook aspects of behaviour which would be immediately apparent to a non-participant observer seeing the situation for the first time.

All that can be said is that, as in the case of interviews, you need to be aware of the dangers and do your best to eliminate preconceived ideas and prejudices. Easier said than done of course. If possible, it is a good idea to ask a colleague (preferably someone who is not a participant) to observe with you and to compare notes afterwards. That at least would provide some check on your interpretation of events.

In 100-hour projects, it would be unwise to undertake unstructured observation unless you are already experienced and are very familiar with the techniques involved. In order to derive worthwhile information from the data, you will probably need to adopt a more structured approach and to devise some form of recording in order to identify aspects of behaviour which you have identified beforehand as being of likely relevance to the research.

This approach can again be criticized as being subjective and biased. You have decided on the focus rather than allowing the focus to emerge. However, you will already have formulated a hypothesis or identified objectives of your study and the importance of observing some aspect of behaviour will have become apparent.

Whether your observation is structured or unstructured and whether you are observing as a participant or a non-participant, your role is to observe and record in as objective a way as possible and then to interpret the data you gather.

Recording and analysing

There are numbers of ways of recording what happens in the class-room or at a meeting, but before a method can be selected a decision has to be made about exactly what is to be observed. This is harder than might at first appear. It is impossible to record everything, so you need to be clear whether you are interested in the *content* or *process* of a lesson or meeting, in *interaction* between individuals, in the *nature of contributions* or in *some specific aspect* such as the effectiveness of questioning techniques. Once you have decided what you wish to find out and have satisfied your-self that you need this information to further your research, then you will be in a position to consider what methods of recording the data will best suit your purposes.

Video and audio recording

In a well-financed project with a team of researchers, it may be possible to record or even to film what is happening in a class or meeting room. However, as with interviews, in a small project there is unlikely to be the money or the time to deal with audio recordings or video tapes. Other methods have to be found which will enable you to record on the spot in an orderly way so that after the event, analysis is quick and easy.

Interaction-process analysis

There are many published observation schedules and accounts of different methods of observing individuals and groups in differ-ent contexts (Flanders 1970, Simon and Boyer 1975, Cohen 1976, Galton 1978, Wragg and Kerry 1978, Williams 1984, 1994, Hop-kins 1985) several of which are based on a system of interaction-process analysis devised by R.F. Bales (1950). Bales's system attempted to describe the behaviour of individuals in groups. He devised a method of classifying or coding, which enabled the observer to record under one of 12 headings which he considered were sufficiently comprehensive to classify different types of behaviour likely to occur in any group. Examples of his categories of behaviour are 'shows tension release' (jokes, laughs, shows satisfaction) and 'shows antagonism' (deflates others' status, defends or asserts self).

Since 1950 many different types of categories have been devised, some relatively simple and others extremely complicated. The Flanders system, which was derived from the Bales method of classifying behaviour, is one of the best known. Flanders (1970) devised ten categories of teacher/student behaviour (the Flanders interaction analysis categories), which the observer used as a basis for categorizing and recording what took place in the classroom. Observers were required to record what was happening every three seconds and to enter the appropriate category number on a prepared chart. The problem about Flanders-type systems is that the categories are quite complex, have numbers of sub-sections and inevitably involve the observer making some value judgements as to which category is closest to particular types of observed behaviour.

The requirement to record every three seconds means that the observer has to be fully conversant with categories and criteria and to recall instantly the number assigned to particular aspects of behaviour. This takes a considerable amount of practice. The more complicated (and so more thorough) the system of categories, the harder it is to manage.

Open University course D101 (now replaced) proposed a much simpler system, though based on similar principles to Bales/Flanders. Students were asked to observe two meetings on an Open University television programme, making use of an abbreviated system devised originally to study management skills and behaviour by the Huthwaite Research Group. Six categories were proposed to help students to classify behaviour in meetings, as follows:

1 Proposing	A behaviour which puts forward a new concept, suggestion or course of action.
2 Supporting	A behaviour which involves a conscious and direct declaration of support or agreement with another person or his or her concepts.

3 Disagreeing	A behaviour which involves a conscious and direct declaration of difference of opinion, or criticism of another person's concepts.
4 Giving information	A behaviour which offers facts, opinions or clarification to other individuals.
5 Seeking information	A behaviour which seeks facts, opinions or clarification from another individual or individuals.
6 Building	A behaviour which extends or develops a proposal which has been made by another person.

These categories describe the kind or style of behaviour engaged in, not the content of what is being said. If you think back to a meeting you have recently attended, you may already envisage difficulties in sorting out one category from another. Several different categories can sometimes be identified within one sentence. A disagreeing statement may also propose, and a supporting statement may also give information. It could be argued that many statements could be categorized as either giving or seeking information. Managing systems of this kind requires practice and careful consideration beforehand about how certain behaviour will be classified, but once the technique has been mastered, it can produce useful data about the behaviour of individuals in groups.

The way in which observations are recorded is largely a matter of personal preference. Using the above categories of behaviour, entries could be made on a table plan, as in Figure 11.1. Numerical entries are made in the appropriate box (e.g. '1' for Proposing, '2' for Supporting, etc.), and the total number of entries listed in whichever format seems most suitable. One way would be to prepare a chart, as shown in Figure 11.2.

Contributions could be plotted on a graph or presented in whichever way illustrated the nature of the contributions made. It would not be enough merely to present the information as observed. Commentary on the significance (or lack of significance) would be necessary and inferences might be drawn about the nature of individual contributions.

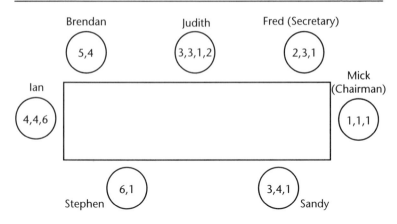

Figure 11.1   Table plan recording individual behaviour according to categories.

Participants	\multicolumn{7}{c}{Categories}
	1	2	3	4	5	6	Totals
Chairman (Mick)	✓✓						③
Secretary (Fred)	✓	✓	✓				③
Judith	✓	✓	✓✓				④
Brendan				✓	✓		②
Ian				✓✓		✓	③
Stephen	✓					✓	②
Sandy	✓		✓	✓			③
Totals	⑦	②	④	④	①	②	

Figure 11.2   Chart recording total number of entries for each behaviour category.

Content

The analysis of the content of a meeting, or consideration of the topics covered, is rather more straightforward. If the main interest was in who made most contributions and spent most time speaking, then a simple chart on the lines shown in Figure 11.3 might be devised. A vertical line would indicate that person spoke for a set time (say half a minute) or less. A following horizontal line would indicate that the same person continued to speak for the same set period.

The previous examples are fairly simple to manage and produce useful, though limited, information. If all you need to know is who spoke most or which topics took up most time, then they will suffice. Adaptations of these charts have been used to good effect in many different situations. However, if you wish to find out who says most about what, then a more complex system is needed, and

Participants	
Mick	/// =
Fred	
Judith	/ = //
Brendan	//
Ian	//// = / =
Stephen	//
Sandy	/ = //
Multiple speaking	///

Figure 11.3 Example of a chart recording speaking contributions by individuals.

it may be best to make fuller notes during the course of the observation and then to transfer to a summary chart.

There are numbers of ways in which such records can be kept. Shaw (1978: 10) suggests that sheets of lined paper should be prepared, marked so that each line represents one minute. The starting time and the topic are entered in a wide vertical margin and every time someone speaks, his or her initials are entered in the margin. A note of the contribution made is entered on the sheet and a line drawn after each topic. Notes are then entered on a summary sheet. This method may not suit you but you need to try out one or two different methods to see which you find easy for recording and for analysis and interpretation after the event.

Selecting a method

Flanders (1970), Simon and Boyer (1975), Cohen (1976), Galton (1978), Wragg and Kerry (1978), Hopkins (1985) and Williams (1994) provide many examples of charts, grids, categories and methods of recording which will give you a range of useful ideas for devising schemes of your own. The sad fact is that in spite of all the tried-and-tested methods that have been employed by experienced researchers over the years, there never seems to be an example that is quite right for the particular task. Inevitably, you will find you have to adapt or to devise a completely new approach, and all new systems need careful piloting and refining in the light of experience. If you have access to only one group or one meeting, you must be quite sure that your selected method of recording is going to work. You will probably need to invent your own system of shorthand symbols and these will have to be memorized. You will need to decide how often to record what is happening (all the time? every three seconds? every five minutes? every twenty minutes?) and with whom (all the group? individuals?) Preparation is all-important. Charts and seating plans have to be prepared. You will need to discuss with the teacher or the chairman of the committee where it would be best to sit. Opinions vary. In a lecture room there is some merit in sitting where the students can see you. At least that way they are not always turning round to see what you are doing, but if the teacher has other views, listen. An observer can never pass entirely un-noticed, but the aim is to be as unobtrusive as possible so that observed behaviour is as close to normal as possible.

Preparation

At the beginning of this chapter, I said that observation can often reveal characteristics of groups or individuals that would have been impossible to discover by other means. This has been demonstrated in many research studies which made extensive use of observation techniques, but the greatest care has to be taken to ensure that you get the most out of the periods of observation. You will not have three years in which to begin an investigation with an entirely open mind and to evolve hypotheses and meth-ods as you go along. It is likely you will have one opportunity only to observe a meeting or a group and so you will need to be quite clear about the purpose of your observation and why you are observing that particular group or individual. You may discover that unforeseen and interesting information emerges during the course of your observation, but you will be mainly dependent on the decisions taken before you begin your period of observation for the type of data you eventually gather. If you make a decision before a meeting that your main interest is the content of the meeting, then charts, grids or checklists have to be devised with that aim in mind. It will be too late to record interactions. If your main interest is process, then other methods will have to be found to record how a lesson or a meeting is conducted. As you select and refine your methods, keep constantly in mind the questions 'What do I need to know?' 'Why do I need to know it?' and 'What shall I do with this information when I have it?' Pilot exercises and practice in recording will answer some of these questions and will point to weaknesses in technique. When you begin your one-off observation exercise, you need to be as sure as you can that you are prepared and ready.

After the event

The task is not complete when the observation has taken place and records have been made. If you were observing a meeting and felt at the end of it that it was rather ineffectual, you would need to analyse the reasons. Was the process altogether too formal? Did the chair speak for 80 per cent of the time? Were contributions from some people dismissed? Some forms of interaction analysis can help you to classify process and content, but whatever methods of recording you have selected, it is essential to consider the event as a whole, as soon after the event as you can. Review in your mind what took place and decide whether any conclusions can be drawn that might be of interest in your study.

Useful though grids, forms and checklists are, they cannot take account of emotions, tensions and hidden agendas. Shaw (1975) in his study of change at St Luke's College of Education used a chart to record interventions in an academic board meeting, but he recognized the limitations of this technique. His subsequent account of the manoeuvring and the lobbying, the anxieties, the delaying tactics and the influence of certain key members of the institution indicates very clearly the importance of the micro-political processes at work in any organization and the effect they can have on the way meetings are conducted and decisions reached.

If you observe a meeting or a group as part of your investigation, make efforts to place what you see in its organizational and/or curricular context, to look beyond the event itself and, in Nisbet's words, 'to spot significant events' (1977: 15).

● Observation studies checklist

1 Decide exactly what you need to know.	List all topics/aspects about which information is required.
2 Consider why you need this information.	Examine your list and remove any item that is not directly associated with the task.
3 Is observation the best way of obtaining the information you need?	Consider alternatives.

4 Decide which aspects you need to investigate.

Are you particularly interested in content, process, interaction, intervention – or something else?

5 Request permission.

Clear official channels and also discuss what is involved with individuals concerned.

6 Devise a suitable grid, checklist or chart.

Consult published examples and adapt where necessary.

7 Consider what you will do with the information.

Is it likely to produce anything of interest? Will the data be sufficiently complete to enable you to come to any conclusions?

8 Pilot your method and revise if necessary.

Memorize categories. Devise your own system of shorthand (symbols, letters, etc.). Practise recording until you are confident you can cope.

9 Prepare carefully before the observation.

Draw a plan of the room, indicating seating arrangements and layout. Make sure you have enough copies of grids or checklists. Consult minutes of previous meetings, agendas, scheme of work, etc.

10 Discuss where you will sit with whoever is in charge and with people who are to be observed.

You want to be as unobtrusive as possible. Exactly where you sit will depend on your own preferences and the views of participants.

11 Remember that no grid, however sophisticated, will tell the full story.

Try to place the event in its organizational context.

12 Analyse and interpret the data.

Factual statements about what has been observed are only part of the task. Consider what the facts indicate or imply.

13 Don't forget to thank the people who have allowed you to observe.

You may need their help again!

Further reading

Several sources are mentioned in the text of this chapter, mainly relating to interaction-process analysis. They are only listed here if they also provide useful guidance about other aspects of observation.

Boehm, A.E. and Weinberg, R.A. (1977) *The Classroom Observer: A Guide for Developing Observation Skills*. New York: Teachers' College Press.

Cohen, L. and Manion, L. (1994) *Research Methods in Education*. London: Routledge. Chapter 5, 'Case studies', provides an excellent introduction to techniques of observation in different settings.

Dixon, B.R., Bouma, G.D. and Atkinson, G.B.J. (1987) *A Handbook of Social Science Research*. Oxford: Oxford University Press. A readable and useful discussion of different approaches. Some good examples of data-recording forms and checklists.

Hopkins, D. (1985) *A Teacher's Guide to Classroom Research*. Milton Keynes: Open University Press. Discusses a series of data-gathering techniques which are of use in observation studies.

Peberdy, A. (1993) 'Observing', Chapter 4 in Shakespeare, P., Atkinson, D. and French, F. (eds) *Reflecting on Research Practice: Issues in Health Care and Social Welfare*. Buckingham: Open University Press.

Shaw, K.E. (1978) *Researching an Organization*. Rediguide 24. University of Nottingham, School of Education. Considers approaches to participant observation.

Spradley, J.P. (1980) *Participant Observation*. New York: Holt, Rinehart & Winston. Charts stages of participant observation and outlines techniques for studying culture.

Williams, G.L. (1984) *Making Your Meetings More Interesting and Effective*. Sheffield City Polytechnic: Pavic Publications.

Williams, G.L. (1984) Chapter 13 in Bell, J. *et al. Conducting Small-scale Investigations in Education Management*. London: Harper & Row. Introduces a range of methods for observing and recording the content and process of meetings. If you decide to observe a meeting, you should read this first.

Williams, G.L. (1994) 'Observing and recording meetings', Chapter 22 in Bennett *et al. Improving Educational Management through Research and Consultancy*. London: Paul Chapman.

 **Part III**

INTERPRETING THE
EVIDENCE AND REPORTING
THE FINDINGS

INTRODUCTION

Data collected by means of questionnaires, interviews, diaries or any other method mean very little until they are analysed and evaluated. Gathering large amounts of information in the hope that something will emerge is not to be recommended in any investigation, but particularly not for researchers who have as little as 100 hours in which to complete a study. As I said in the Introduction at the beginning of this book, those of you who have a limited statistical background cannot attempt highly complex surveys involving advanced statistical techniques, but that does not mean that a worthwhile study cannot be carried out. It is all a case of working within your limitations and selecting research methods which are suitable for the task and which can be readily analysed, interpreted and presented.

If at some stage you decide to carry out a large quantitative study, then you will undoubtedly need to get to grips with statistical procedures and with a range of computer skills and computer software such as the Statistical Package for the Social Sciences (SPSS). Every institution of higher education should have specialists who will advise. Make use of them. They will keep you on the straight and narrow and will ensure you do not waste valuable time following false trails.

In most 100-hour projects, it will be sufficient to understand simple arithmetical procedures such as averages and percentages.

If your data-collecting instruments are well devised and have been well piloted, you have already done the groundwork for the collation, analysis and presentation of information.

Before you begin your study of the next two chapters there are a number of issues which have been raised earlier but which need to be reiterated. In Chapter 1, I briefly discussed the question of generalization. Bassey (1981: 85–6) drew attention to the problems of generalizing from insufficient data, and made a strong case for individual researchers working to a limited time scale to produce research structured in response to an existing or potential problem so that the results might be of use to the institution. Such research, he felt, might go some way to solving a particular problem or lead to informed discussion of how a particular problem might be tackled. He commended the descriptive and evaluative study of single pedagogic events and (writing about case-study methods), concluded that

> an important criterion for judging the merit of a case study is the extent to which the details are sufficient and appropriate for a teacher working in a similar situation to relate his decision-making to that described in the case study. The relatability of a case study is more important than its generalizability.
>
> (Bassey 1981: 85)

I raise this issue again here because in the analysis, interpretation and presentation of data, care has to be taken not to claim more for results than is warranted, and equal care has to be taken not to attempt generalizations based on insufficient data. In a 100-hour project, generalization may be unlikely, but relatability may be entirely possible. Well-prepared, small-scale studies may inform, illuminate and provide a basis for policy decisions within the institution. As such, they can be invaluable. There is no need to apologize about inability to generalize, but there would be every need to apologize if data were manipulated in an attempt to prove more than could reasonably be claimed.

12

INTERPRETATION AND PRESENTATION OF THE EVIDENCE

Raw data taken from questionnaires, interview schedules, check-lists, etc. need to be recorded, analysed and interpreted. A hundred separate pieces of interesting information will mean nothing to a researcher or to a reader unless they have been placed into categories. We are constantly looking for similarities and differences, for groupings, patterns and items of particular significance

You may have ideas about categories before the data are collected. Your informed hunch tells you that the likelihood is that responses will tend to fall into any one of six or seven main categories. There can be dangers in placing too much reliance on preconceived ideas, not least the possibility that your line of questioning may direct students to reply in certain ways. However, assuming you have been able to eliminate bias of this kind, your first-thoughts categories will give you a start in the process of collating the findings. Other categories will undoubtedly emerge as your collation proceeds.

In Chapter 8, Michael Youngman suggested that in questionnaires, it is helpful to identify question types and to work out ways in which responses can be analysed and presented. You will recall that he listed seven question types (list, category, ranking, scale, quantity, grid and verbal). In this chapter, some of these question types will be used to illustrate ways in which responses might be interpreted and presented.

List questions

Let us say you wish to find out what qualifications your mature students had before they registered for the course. You produce a list question which invites subjects to tick appropriate boxes. They may well tick more than one box and so you will need to be ready to deal with multiple responses. In Question 1, categories have already been selected (None, O level/GCSE, Access and A level) which makes collation simple. If responses to the 'Other' question fall into convenient groups, then you will add other categories but if responses produce a very varied list, you may decide to settle for grouping them as 'Other qualifications'.

Question 1

What qualifications did you have before you started your degree course?
(Please tick the appropriate box or boxes)

None ☐   Successful completion ☐
                  of Access or Return
                  to Study course

GCE O level/GCSE ☐   GCE A level ☐

Other (please specify) _____
_____
_____

A summary sheet needs to be prepared for all questions before questionnaires are distributed, so that returns can be entered as they come in. We all have our own ways of recording returns, but if you decide to record question by question, the following is probably as simple a way as any.

Summary sheet for Question 1

Question 1 Qualifications before entry				
None	*O level/GCSE*	*A level*	*Access/Return to Study*	*Other*
‖‖‖ ‖	‖‖‖ ‖‖‖ ‖‖‖ ‖‖‖ ‖‖‖ ‖‖	‖‖‖ ‖‖‖ ‖‖	‖‖‖ ‖‖‖ ‖‖‖ ‖‖‖ ‖‖‖ ‖‖‖ ‖‖	‖‖‖ ‖‖‖ ‖‖‖ ‖
6	28	12	32	16

Once the summary sheet is complete, you will begin to have a picture of the types of qualifications the students had before beginning their degree course. The information can be presented in a variety of ways. A simple table, followed by commentary highlighting any items of interest is one option.

Table 12.1 Qualifications of mature students before entry to their degree course

None	*O level/GCSE*	*A level*	*Access/Return to Study*	*Other*
6	28	12	32	16

The full list of 'Other' qualifications will need to be recorded on a separate sheet and if categories of qualification emerge, then reference can be made to them in the commentary.

A vertical bar chart would be another option. The variable (qualification) would be on the horizontal axis and the frequency (number of students) on the vertical axis. (Note that 'n' = number.)

Which is the clearer? The table or the bar chart? Any data which

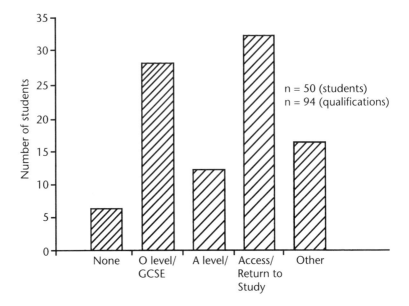

Figure 12.1 Qualifications of students before entry to their degree course.

tell you nothing of significance may as well be abandoned, but there are interesting features here. Thirty-two of the 50 students in our sample (64 per cent) took Access/Return to Study courses, whereas only 12 (24 per cent) had A levels. It might be interesting to discover which group performed better in examinations. Six students (12 per cent of the total of 50) had no qualifications on entry at all. How then had they prepared themselves for their undergraduate studies? Are they coping? It might be useful to follow up these and similar issues in interviews.

Category questions

What Michael Youngman described as category questions are, at first sight, simpler to deal with. They require one answer only. If subjects are asked how old they are, they give only one answer. In the mature students' study, you will probably need to know students' ages. If you have spent time on question wording and have refined the focus of each question, you will have decided whether you want to know students' ages at the time they registered, at the time they completed the questionnaire, or at some other stage. You decide to ask a straight question.

Question 2

> **How old were you when you first registered for your degree course?**

What will you do with responses? *What exactly do you want to know?* The average age of students? If so, you will need to decide what sort of average (or measure of central tendency) will suit your purpose – *the arithmetic mean, the median,* or *the mode.*

The arithmetic mean is simple. It is obtained by adding together each item (or value) and dividing by the total number of values. So if we take 12 subjects (Group A) whose ages are 26, 26, 27, 28, 29, 30, 30, 31, 32, 33, 34, 34, and add those values together: that gives us 360. Divide 360 by 12. The mean is 30.

Another group of 12 (Group B) might have a different range of ages. For example, 21, 22, 24, 25, 25, 29, 31, 31, 32, 35, 40 and 45. The mean age is also 30. In these two cases, there is a clear difference in the dispersion of results.

The median allows us to find the middle value. This is particularly useful when there are extremes at both ends or at either end of the range which may affect the mean to a significant extent. To find the median, values must be listed in order – which in this case has already been done. If we had an odd number of values, the middle value would be the median. Where we have an even number, as in Group A, the average of the two middle values (30 + 30) is taken and so 30 is the median. The fact that in this case the mean and the median are the same is because there are no extreme values at either end. There is an age progression, but if the ages were 21, 22, 29, 30, 30, 33, 33, 33, 36, 84, then the differences would become apparent. The mean would be 35.1, whereas the median would be the average of the middle points, which would be 31.5. You would then need to decide whether the median gives a more realistic picture than the mean.

The mode, which is not often used in small studies, relates to the most frequently occurring value. In this last example, the modal score is 33.

Each of these measures of central tendency has different uses. As always, it all depends on what you need to know and why.

Look at the Group A and Group B examples again. The two groups have a very different spread of age. In Group A, the range is from 26 to 34 and so ages are close to the mean and the median. In Group B, they range from 21 to 45 and so are not clustered around the mean age. Is that worthy of comment? If so, ways have to be found of dealing with measures of spread, or dispersion. Commonly used measures are *range, interquartile range* and *standard deviation*.

Range is simply the difference between the highest and lowest values measured. For Group A, the range is 8 years, but for Group B it is 24 years. The range is not a particularly good measure of dispersion, as it can be influenced by one high and/or one low value and takes no account of the numbers of responses in the middle of the group.

The interquartile range gives a more accurate picture and reduces the importance of the extreme ends of the range. It is derived from the *median*. The highest quarter and the lowest quarter of the measures are omitted and the interquartile range of the middle 50 per cent of values is quoted.

For Group A, the top three values (34, 34 and 33 – one quarter of the twelve values) are omitted, as are the lowest three values (26, 26 and 27). This gives an interquartile range of 28–32, or four years.

For Group B, the values 45, 40 and 35 are omitted, as are 21, 22 and 24. That gives an interquartile range of 25–32, which is seven years. Is that worth commenting on? In some cases, it certainly will be. If the median has been selected as providing the best indication of the average of a set of data, then the interquartile range will indicate the extent to which data vary.

If the mean has been selected, then the *standard deviation* has to be used to summarize dispersion. It reflects the spread and the degree to which the values differ from the mean. It uses values for all the group rather than for a section, whereas other measures do not. Any book on statistics will give the mathematical expression for standard deviation and how it can be calculated. To carry out the calculations by hand can be tedious, particularly for a large group. However, some calculators can do this very quickly and the calculation is written into many computer programs so that the standard deviation is automatically produced in association with the mean. In fact, the standard deviation for Group A is 2.8 and for Group B it is 7.

In the case of these two groups, all the measures – the range, interquartile range and standard deviation – indicate that Group B has a wider spread than Group A. Used on their own, means and medians may not be sufficiently descriptive to provide a complete picture of the data. You will need to decide whether one of these measures of dispersion is also necessary when you analyse and interpret your data.

It was a straightforward matter to determine the mean and the median of data derived from Question 2. However, you might decide you do not wish to ask subjects to say how old they are. Perhaps you consider it would be more sensitive to ask them to tick a box or circle a number to indicate the age category into which they fit. Decide whether you wish to have categories (or class intervals) of five (20–24, 25–29) or ten (20–29, 30–39). How important is it to have the groups of five? If the answer is 'not very', then take the wider span. It will be easier to manage.

Make sure your instructions are clear. In the Alternative Question 2, respondents would be asked to circle the number (1–5) under the appropriate age category. A respondent of 32 would circle the number 2 underneath the 30–39 age category. Take particular care to ensure that the likely full age range of your subjects is provided.

Alternative Question 2

Age when you first registered for your degree				
20–29	30–39	40–49	50–59	60+
1	②	3	4	5

If you wished to find the arithmetic means of respondents' ages from the class intervals, this is still straightforward. Take the mid-point of each class interval and multiply that age by the number in each class. That is, mid-point × frequency, as follows:

Age	Frequency	Mid-point	Frequency × Mid-point
20–29	34	25	850
30–39	10	35	350
40–49	4	45	180
50–59	1	55	55
60+	1	60	60
Total	50		1495

If 1495 is divided by the number of subjects (50), that gives a mean of 29.9. The first class interval (20–29) includes those who entered higher education on their twentieth birthday and also those who entered the day before their thirtieth birtday. The interval therefore covers almost 10 years, so the most accurate mid-point is 25 (not 24.5, which is the mean of 20 and 29). The following intervals also cover 10 years, with the exception of the final class (60+). Usually, it is anticipated that only a small number of responses will fall into the final class. In the above example, the one respondent could be any age from 60 upwards and so it is

Table 12.2   Age distribution of students at the start of their course

Age	Number of students
20–29	34
30–39	10
40–49	4
50–59	1
60+	1
Total	50

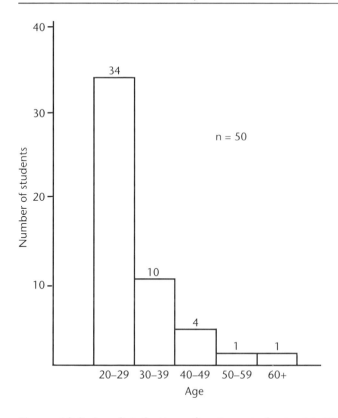

Figure 12.2 Age distribution of mature students at initial registration.

necessary to assign an arbitrary mid-point. For the purpose of this exercise, the age 60 was selected.

You would then need to decide how to present the information in a way which best illustrates the age balance of the sample. You have several options. You could provide a simple chart derived straight from your summary sheet (Table 12.2).

The same data could be represented by a histogram. A histogram is the same as a bar chart, but the bars are touching, to reflect the continuous nature of the variable which in this case is 'age' (Figure 12.2).

Alternatively, you might decide a pie chart would present a

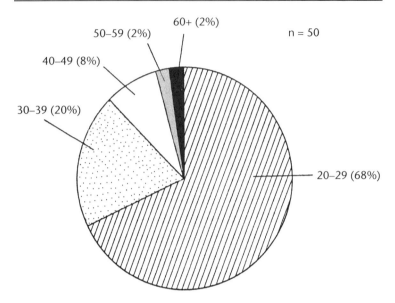

Figure 12.3 Age distribution of students at the start of their course.

clearer (or different) picture. Pie charts can be awkward to draw unless you have access to a computer graphics program, but they are useful, particularly if you wish to illustrate the *proportion* of students who fall into the different age groups. In this case, frequencies are first changed to percentages. The 30–39 age range accounts for 20 per cent of the total sample. The circumference of a circle is 360° and so 1 per cent will be 3.6°. Multiply 20 by 3.6 which gives 72°. This simple calculation will allow you to draw in the segments using a protractor and a compass. As numbers are small, it is as well to indicate numbers in addition to percentages (Figure 12.3).

Do the table, the histogram or the pie chart provide any interesting findings? You might comment on this skewed age distribution, to the effect that few students over the age of 39 had committed themselves to the three-year full time undergraduate course. But why would that be interesting? Subsequent interviews might provide further information about motives. Would you have expected the age distribution to be weighted at the younger end? When you examine the university records for the full mature student population (assuming you have permission to get access to the records), does your sample follow the same pattern, or is it different? If it is significantly different, then that might indicate that further study is needed to try to find why. Do university records indicate a gradual (or sudden) change in the age profile of students? What about the balance of women to men? Would it be helpful to know whether most of the younger students are men and most of the older students are women? If you have asked students to indicate whether they are male or female, you would be able to find that out, but if you have not, it will be too late once the questionnaires are returned.

Your pilot and trial collation and presentation of data should give you clues as to which information is likely to be of interest and at that stage there is still time to make adjustments to your data-collecting instruments. The trials will also allow you to prepare the types of summary sheets which will suit your purpose.

The simple summary sheet I suggested for Question 1 will suffice if you wish to record on a question-by-question basis, but it is often desirable to deal with returns on a questionnaire-by-questionnaire basis. Data in Question 1 and Alternative Question 2 are already grouped, and it is easy to code each response (that is, to give a number to each category). So, in Question 1, coding could be on the following lines:

No qualifications   1
GCE O level/GCSE etc.   2

In Question 2 and Alternative Question 2, codes would be allocated in the same way:

20–29   1
30–39   2

A summary sheet could then be devised as follows:

Summary sheet for Questions 1, 2, etc.

Student number	Question 1					Question 2					Question 3 etc.
	1	2	3	4	5	1	2	3	4	5	
1	✓						✓				
2	✓		✓					✓			
3			✓			✓			✓		
Etc.											

From a chart of this kind, it is easy to produce total responses to each question or part of question. Recording responses is time-consuming, but if the charts are prepared beforehand and are well devised, it makes collation straightforward. A summary sheet on the above lines, adjusted to suit your particular needs, will mean that questionnaires can be put to one side once all entries are made. You may need to refer to them periodically, but the majority of the information you will need for collation, analysis and presentation will be on the summary sheets.

Grids

The simple response questions such as list and category questions are relatively easy to deal with. Grids require a little more care. A grid (or table) question will ask students to provide answers to two or more questions at the same time.

Go back to the question about students' qualifications before they started their degree course. Instead of merely asking whether they had no qualifications, GCE O level/GCSE, GCE A levels, or had successfully completed an Access or other course, you might decide it would be more useful to learn about study carried out after the age of 18. If so, a grid question could be devised.

Question 3

Since the age of 18, how many years have you spent on the following? Ignore periods of less than one academic year.

	1–2 years	3–4 years	5–6 years	More than 6 years
GCE O level or GCSE				
GCE A level				
Access/Return to Study course/s				
No formal study				
Other (please specify)				

Here there are two dimensions – years of study and type of study. Students might have spent one year on O level or GCSE, two years on a Return to Study course and five years on nursing qualifications. In that case, ticks would be placed in three boxes.

The returns could be presented in table form in much the same style as the original question, but it would also be possible to produce a compound bar chart which compares numbers of students by years of study spent on different courses (see Figure 12.4).

Scales

The examples so far ask respondents to give factual information. *Scales* are devices to discover strength of feeling or attitude. There are many different types of scale, some of which require quite complex construction and analysis. Thurstone and Guttman scales in particular require careful handling. The most straight-

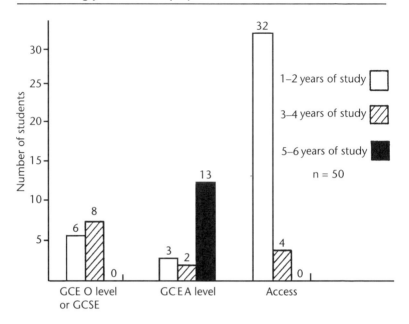

Figure 12.4 Years spent on study since the age of 18.

forward attitude scale is probably the Likert. Likert scales ask respondents to indicate strength of agreement or disagreement with a given statement or series of statements on a five- or seven-point range. Answers are then scored, generally from 1 (strongly disagree) to 5 (strongly agree) and a measure of respondents' feelings can be produced.

A simplified Likert scale might be used in the following case:

Question 4

I consider my chances of doing well in finals are good				
Strongly disagree	*Disagree*	*Undecided*	*Agree*	*Strongly agree*
1	2	3	4	5

Responses could be presented as shown in Table 12.3.

Table 12.3 Levels of agreement among mature students that chances of success in finals are good

Strongly disagree	Disagree	Undecided	Agree	Strongly agree	Totals
10	7	6	16	11	50
(20%)	(14%)	(12%)	(32%)	(22%)	(100%)

A bar chart would also illustrate the range of responses, as in Figure 12.5.

It is clear from Table 12.3 and from the bar chart (Figure 12.5) that more than half the students (54 per cent) are optimistic about their results, but what about the rest? Will these percentages be influenced by the faculty to which students belong? It would be interesting to find out.

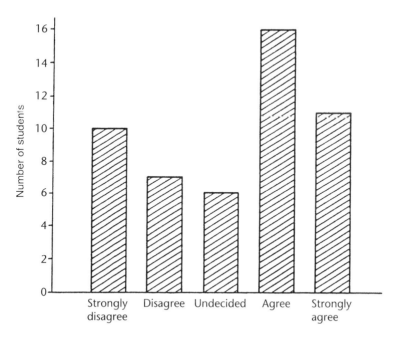

Figure 12.5 Levels of agreement among mature students (n = 50) that chances of success in finals are good.

Early findings from the pilot study may have alerted you to the likely importance of the faculty dimension. If so, you would have been able to ask students to complete a combined Likert scale/grid question, which might produce the results shown in Table 12.4.

Table 12.4 Levels of agreement among mature students that chances of success, by faculty, are good

Faculty	Strongly disagree	Disagree	Undecided	Agree	Strongly agree	Total
Maths	4	0	0	0	0	4
Science	6	6	2	0	0	14
Social Science	0	0	4	16	0	20
Humanities	0	1	0	0	11	12
Totals	10	7	6	16	11	50

Presenting these data in tabular form is perfectly acceptable, but ask yourself whether other methods of presentation would illustrate the position more clearly. In this case, numbers may not present the same picture as would percentages, though in small studies it is dangerous to use percentages without the associated numbers. They can be misleading and give the impression that the sample is bigger than it in fact is. However, if you decide it is likely to be important to know the proportion of students who disagree or agree with the statement *by faculty*, then frequencies can be converted to percentages and a percentage component bar chart produced (Figure 12.6).

Does Figure 12.6 illustrate the position better? You will need to decide. What does emerge is that the table and the bar chart make it clear that there are major differences in the perceptions of Maths and Science students compared with Social Science and Humanities. The percentage component bar chart demonstrates the extent of the differences. So, what is happening in Maths and Science? Were the students inadequately prepared? Are there

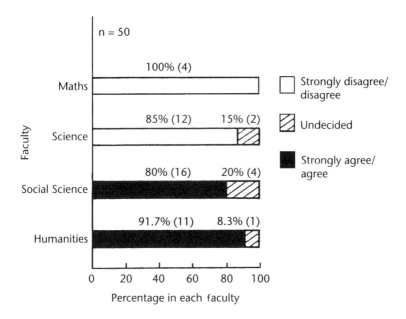

Figure 12.6 Percentage of students by faculty who feel their chances of doing well in finals are good.

lessons to be learnt from these data? Or are the students unnecessarily pessimistic about their prospects? All these questions could be followed up in interviews with students and with tutors.

The table and bar chart illustrate the extent to which there is a relationship between faculty and students' perceptions of chances of success in finals.

Data plotted onto a scattergram (or scattergraph) may also indicate a relationship between two variables.

As part of your investigation, you may have hypothesized that first-year coursework scores will be related to first-year examination scores. Unlikely though it would be, you might find the scores given in Table 12.5.

It is obvious that both scores match exactly. If these data are plotted on a graph, with the examination score as the horizontal axis and the coursework score on the vertical axis, then a perfect straight line is produced, as in Figure 12.7.

Table 12.5 First-year examination and coursework scores (1)

Student number	Examination score	Coursework score
1	30	30
2	35	35
3	40	40
4	45	45
5	50	50
6	55	55
7	60	60
8	65	65
9	70	70

(If you produce the graph by hand, it is easier if you use graph paper.) The increase in examination score is matched by an increase in coursework score and therefore the results are said to correlate positively.

Because a proportionate increase in examination score is associated with an equal proportionate increase in coursework score, a 'perfect' positive correlation between the variables is achieved.

Another sample might produce different data (Table 12.6).

These data, transferred onto a graph (Figure 12.8) demonstrate that again, the correlation is 'perfect', but this time, as the examination score increases, the coursework decreases, and vice

Table 12.6 First-year examination and coursework scores (2)

Student number	Examination score	Coursework score
1	30	70
2	35	65
3	40	60
4	45	55
5	50	50
6	55	45
7	60	40
8	65	35
9	70	30

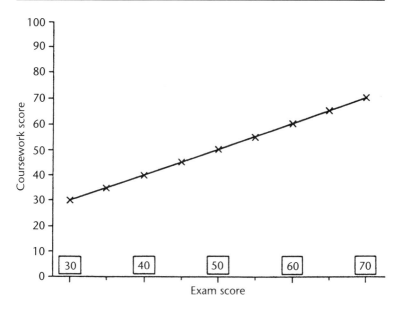

Figure 12.7 Positive relationship between examination and coursework scores.

versa. There is, therefore, a negative relationship between the two variables. In reality, such relationships are rare. More realistic data might be as in Table 12.7.

When the points are plotted on the graph, the resulting figure

Table 12.7 First-year examination and coursework scores (3)

Student number	Examination score	Coursework score
1	37	45
2	42	40
3	46	44
4	53	68
5	54	60
6	59	50
7	63	55
8	72	85
9	74	75

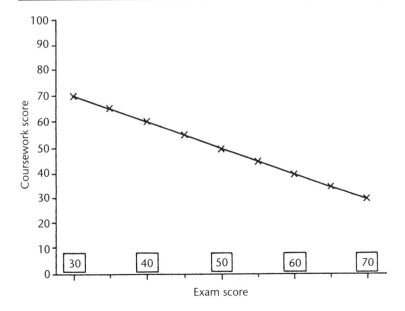

Figure 12.8 Negative relationship between examination and coursework scores.

(Figure 12.9) shows whether there is a general trend in the results and indicates the scatter of results. In this case, since the general trend is for an increase in examination score associated with an increase in coursework score, a positive relationship exists, but it is not perfect.

Some data, when plotted on a scattergram, may be completely random, with no discernible pattern. In this case, it is reasonable to assume that there is little or no relationship between variables. In other cases, there may be clusters, or groups of points on the scattergram, suggesting that within the total sample, there are smaller groups within which the individuals have similar characteristics. Take care though. Unless calculations for correlation coefficients are carried out, only inferences can be drawn – not direct causal relationships. If you feel correlation coefficients are necessary then you will have to become familiar with the necessary statistical techniques or to make use of a Statistical Package for the Social Sciences (SPSS) package.

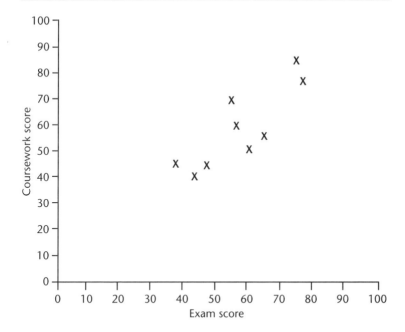

Figure 12.9 Positive (though not perfect) relationship between examination and coursework scores.

Verbal questions

A study of responses to verbal (or open) questions will often provide useful pointers to the types of issues it may be worthwhile to follow up in interviews. These questions are often included on questionnaires to allow respondents to draw attention to anything about which they feel strongly. Referring to such responses is often a way of starting an interview.

The usual practice is to write or type out all the responses onto separate sheets. This allows all items to be scanned in order to see whether there are any recurring themes. If you are interested in discovering whether students identify any barriers to learning, you will be looking particularly to statements which relate to problems with study, tutor support, etc. Some of the responses will probably provide useful quotations to illustrate certain points in the report – though the temptation to give greater emphasis to statements which happen to support your particular point of view has to be resisted.

Michael Youngman (Chapter 8) suggests that some form of content analysis may be necessary in order to deal with such material. You will in fact follow the same content analysis procedures as would be applied for the study of documents (see Chapter 7). As always, you will be looking for categories and for common criteria, if any.

Conclusions

Only the simplest methods of presentation have been considered in this chapter. They provide a starting point. The tables and charts are easy to manage, whether or not you have access to a computer graphics program. You may be able to devise different question types and different methods of analysis and presentation. The advantage of familiarizing yourself with a range of question types is that once you have experimented with different formats and know how to produce tables, charts or graphs, you will be able to draw on whichever format suits the data and the purpose. A diagram can often simplify quite complex data which could take a paragraph or more to explain.

When you wish to move on to larger and more complex investigations, you will need to familiarize yourself with more complex methods of analysis and with the use of appropriate computer programs. If you have access to a computer centre, you may wish to try out some of the SPSS programs, using data with which you are familiar – possibly data which have been collated, analysed and presented 'by hand' in connection with one of your 100-hour projects. This will allow you to understand the principles and to get to grips with the practicalities of the system.

⦿ **Interpretation and presentation of the evidence checklist**

1 Data must be recorded, analysed and interpreted.

2 Look for similarities, groupings and items of particular significance.

Identify categories.

3 First-thoughts categories will be a start in the process of collating findings.

4 Prepare summary sheets.

Enter responses as returns are received.

5 Experiment with different ways of presenting findings.

Table? Bar chart? Histogram? Other diagrams or graphs?

6 If you need to discover the average of certain values, decide whether the mean, median or mode is the most suitable.

Remember that each of these measures of central tendency has different uses.

7 Used on their own, means and medians may not be sufficiently descriptive to provide a complete picture of the data.

A measure of dispersion may be required – range, interquartile range or standard deviation.

8 All data require interpretation.

It is not enough only to describe.

9 Try out different methods of presentation for responses to different question types.

Select whichever best illustrates the point/s you are making.

10 Do not attempt complex statistical techniques unless you have the expertise to cope.

It is perfectly possible to produce a worthwhile investigation without an in-depth knowledge of statistics and without access to a computer.

Further reading

There are many books on the market now which deal with basic statistical techniques. If you feel you need to learn more, ask at your local library or bookshop, consult the introduction and the contents page to see whether your understanding of 'basic' is the same as the author's. Other sources are:

Bryman, A. and Cramer, D. (1990) *Quantitative Data Analysis for Social Scientists*. London: Routledge. Of interest to anyone who wishes to learn more about analysing data with computers, in particular the use of SPSS. Quite the best and most readable book on this topic (though some basic statistical know-how does help).

Coolican, H. (1994) *Research Methods and Statistics in Psychology*, 2nd edn. London: Routledge.

Dixon, B.R., Bouma, G.D. and Atkinson, G.B.J. (1987) *A Handbook of Social Science Research*. Oxford: Oxford University Press. An easy-to-read and helpful book. Useful chapters on 'Collecting data' (Chapter 8) and 'Summarising and presenting data' (Chapter 9).

Goulding, S. (1984) 'Analysis and presentation of information', Chapter 11 in Bell, J. *et al. Conducting Small-scale Investigations in Educational Management*. London: Harper & Row.

Healey, J.F. and Earl, R.B. (1997) *SPSS for Windows: Exploring Social Issues Using SPSS for Windows*. London: Pineforge Press.

Holsti, O.R. (1969) *Content Analysis for the Social Sciences and Humanities*. Reading, MA: Addison-Wesley. Rather old now, but still regarded as a standard work on content analysis. Perhaps rather detailed for small-scale studies.

Howard, K. and Sharpe, J.A. (1983) *The Management of a Student Research Project*. Aldershot: Gower. Chapter 5 'Analysing the data' and Chapter 6 'Gathering the data' are useful.

Kinnear, P.R. and Gray, C.D. (1994) *SPSS for Windows made Simple*. Hove: Laurence Erlbaum.

Marsh, C. (1988) *Exploring Data: An Introduction to Data Analysis for Social Sciences*. London: Polity Press. Assumes some social-science background, but provides helpful guidance about analysis and presentation.

Moser, C.A. and Kalton, G. (1971) *Survey Methods in Social Investigation*, 2nd edn. London: Heinemann. This is an essential source of guidance about planning surveys, including sampling, scaling methods, analysis, interpretation and the presentation of data.

Oppenheim, A.N. (1966) *Questionnaire Design and Attitude Measurement*. London: Heinemann. Useful section on the construction of coding frames which will be essential in larger investigations. Chapter 6, 'Attitude-scaling methods' and Chapter 9 'The quantification of questionnaire data' are well worth considering.

SPSS (1990) *SPSS User's Guide*. Chicago: SPSS Inc.

SPSS (1990) *SPSS Categories*. Chicago: SPSS Inc.

Strauss, A. (1987) *Qualitative Analysis for Social Scientists*. Cambridge: Cambridge University Press. As the title indicates, this book discusses a range of techniques designed to analyse qualitative data. Should be used as a reference book, but full of helpful advice about interpretation and analysis.

13

WRITING THE REPORT

Getting started

When all the hard work of gathering and analysing evidence is complete, you will need to write the final report. Bogdan and Biklen, writing about the problems of getting started, offer the following advice:

> Novice writers are big procrastinators. They find countless reasons not to get started. Even when they finally get themselves seated at their desks, they always seem to find diversions: make the coffee, sharpen the pencil, go to the bathroom, thumb through more literature, sometimes even get up and return to the field. Remember that you are never 'ready' to write; writing is something you must make a conscious decision to do and then discipline yourself to follow through.
>
> (Bogdan and Biklen 1982: 172)

All this is easier said than done, and it is not only novice writers who are procrastinators, but remember that a study is not finished until it is written up and, in your original planning, time has to be allowed for writing. That does not mean that you put off thoughts of writing until all the data have been collected. If you have followed some of the earlier advice, you will already have produced an evaluation of what you have read about the topic, so you will not have to waste time going back to books and articles read some time ago. You will have your bibliographical cards and/or computer records in good order, with notes and useful quotations to guide your writing, and you will not have started your project unless your objectives were clear, though you may have amended your objectives as your investigation developed.

Report and thesis writing is not, or should not be, a frantic activity carried out at the end of the project. It is a process of varied stages all of which need to be recorded at the time they are completed. Your first drafts will almost certainly need to be revised and in some cases completely rewritten, but the foundations for the report should have been established at the planning stage.

Writing a report or a dissertation requires discipline, and even the most experienced of researchers needs to impose some sort of self-control to ensure that the task is completed on time. We all have different ways of working and what suits one person may not suit another. By a method of trial and error, you will need to work out what is best for you, but the following guidelines, which derive largely from Barzun and Graff (1977), may provide a starting point for working out your own writing plan:

1 *Set deadlines:* You will already have set deadlines and completion dates for different sections and for the whole report in your original schedule, but plans and ideas do sometimes change during the course of an investigation. With the help of your supervisor, set a deadline for the completion of the writing and keep that date constantly in mind.
2 *Write regularly:* Many researchers find that they need to keep regular hours and to work in the same place. They find that building up an association between work and a particular place eases the difficulty of starting to write. The aim is never to miss a writing session.
3 *Create a rhythm of work:* Barzun and Graff (1977: 325) suggest that the periods of writing should be 'close enough to create a rhythm of work'. It is tempting to stop to check a reference or because you have written a certain number of words that would seem to justify breaking off at that point, but resist the temptation. Keep the momentum going.

4 *Write up a section as soon as it is ready:* Some sections of the research will be ready for writing before others. Whatever sequence is attempted, it is a good idea to aim at writing a minimum number of words in each writing session.

5 *Stop at a point from which it is easy to resume writing:* If you stop at a point when the next passage is difficult, it may discourage you from resuming work promptly for the next session. It is better to stop at a point when the next session's writing can get off to a running start.

6 *Leave space for revisions:* You will almost certainly need to revise and rewrite, so write only one paragraph on each page so that you can move paragraphs around if necessary. Remember also to write on only one side of each page.

7 *Publicize your plans:* You may need some help from family and friends to complete your report on time. We can all find good reasons for not getting down to writing, so tell everyone about your writing routine. With any luck, they will not tempt you with invitations to the pub or incite you to watch television. They may in fact put pressure on you to get to your desk. As Barzun and Graff (1977: 325) emphasize, 'The writer's problem is the inverse of the reformed drunkard's. The latter must never touch a drop; the former must always do his stint.'

Structuring the report

All institutions should provide guidelines about the way the final report should be structured and it goes without saying that these guidelines should be followed to the letter. If for any reason guidelines are not provided, the following format will generally be acceptable.

1 Title page

Include the title of your study, your name and the date. The title should accurately reflect the nature of your study and should be brief and to the point. A subtitle may be provided if it clarifies the purpose of the study.

2 Acknowledgements

You may wish to acknowledge the help given to you in the preparation of your report. If so, acknowledgements and thanks generally come after the title page.

3 Contents

4 The abstract

In most cases, an abstract will be required, though practices vary, so consult the 'house' rules. It is quite difficult to say in a few words what your investigation set out to do, the methods employed and what conclusions were reached. The following example is one way in which the task might be approached.

> This project attempts to identify effective teaching and learning strategies and any barriers to learning as perceived by mature students at Bramhope University. Data were gathered from questionnaires, interviews and observation of and participation in lectures, seminars and tutorials. The report concludes that there is scope for consideration of more varied approaches to the delivery of the curriculum and for consultations with mature students about ways in which changes might be introduced.

If you are allowed more space, you would be able to develop this abstract to provide the reader with more information, but for short reports, something on the above lines will generally suffice.

5 Aims and purpose of the study

This should be a brief explanation of the purpose of the research. Explain the research problem in a few sentences. State aims/objectives/hypotheses. Provide any background to the study which is necessary to place the study in its context.

Draw attention to any limitations of the study at this stage. An individual researcher with only 100 hours or so to complete a project can hope neither to become involved in complex sampling techniques nor to interview hundreds of people. You cannot do everything in a small study, and your supervisor will know that, but in this section you should make it clear that you know what the limitations of the study are.

6 Review of the literature

Not all reports will include a review of previous research, though most will. You may have used your background reading mainly to support arguments throughout the report, but the value of a review to the reader is that it explains the context and background of the study. Remember Haywood and Wragg's warning that critical reviews can too often turn out to be uncritical reviews – 'the furniture sale catalogue, in which everything merits a one-paragraph entry no matter how skilfully it has been conducted' (Haywood and Wragg 1982: 2). Selection has to be made, and only books and articles which relate directly to the topic should be included. Do you recall Woodley's (1985) review of the literature relating to mature students, discussed in Chapter 6. He selected from an extensive amount of literature only material which related to his own study. He grouped certain categories, commented on features which were of particular importance, compared the results of different investigations and discussed in some detail a study by Walker (1975), which served as a pilot study for his own research. In his review of the literature, he set the scene, placed his own work in context and prepared the reader for what was to follow.

The literature review can be written first and, if you have managed to discipline yourself sufficiently well to write up sections and sub-sections as you have completed them, much of the work of this section will be ready for revision before you begin to collect data. You may find that you need to adapt your original version, but you should not need to start from the beginning by reading through notes to decide what should be included and what left out.

Clara Nai adopted this approach. She identified headings under which she could group her findings and in so doing, produced an analytical framework which enabled her to highlight key issues and, at a later stage in her dissertation, to place her own research findings into the wider context.

7 Methodology

An alternative heading might be 'Some considerations of method' – or any other title which in your view describes the content of the section well. This section explains how the problem was investigated and why particular methods and techniques were employed. Accounts of the procedure, size of sample, method of selection, choice of variables and controls, and tests of measurement and statistical analysis, if any, should be provided.

Nisbet and Entwistle (1970: 169) point out that it is unnecessary to describe in detail any standard tests or procedures that are well known and about which further information can easily be obtained, but if subjective assessments or individually devised measurement techniques have been used, then some explanation is necessary.

All important terms should be defined precisely and any deficiencies in the methods mentioned. It is important to bear in mind that in certain kinds of investigation, the research needs to be repeatable, and a fellow researcher should be able to obtain enough information from this section to make this possible.

8 Statement of results

This is the heart of the report and will consist of tables or figures and text, depending on the nature of the project. The way results are presented is important. Tables, charts, graphs and other figures should illustrate and illuminate the text. If they do not, then there is no point in taking up space. The text, which should be written after the results are prepared, should not duplicate information in the tables and figures but should highlight significant aspects of the findings so that all relevant facts are presented in a way which draws the reader's attention to what is most important. It is quite an art to achieve this balance, and you may find you need several drafts before you are satisfied with the result.

All tables and figures should be numbered, given a title and carefully checked before you submit your report. Tables are generally numerical presentations, in lists or columns, though there can be tables of names or other items. Figures are other types of presentation of data. It is quite a good idea to look at the way other students have presented them and take care to follow any institutional guidelines.

9 Analysis and discussion

It is often best to start this section with a restatement of the problem before discussing how the results affect existing knowledge of the subject. If your research aimed to test certain hypotheses, then this section should demonstrate whether they were or were not supported by the evidence. Any deficiencies in the research design should be mentioned, with suggestions about different approaches which might have been more appropriate. Implications for improvement of practice, if any, should also be drawn out.

Most researchers find it best to write sections 6, 7 and 8 in sequence to ensure continuity and logical progression. It is quite feasible to write some sections as discrete units at different times, but these three sections need to be considered as a whole. If you have to take a break from writing, make sure you reread everything that has gone before to ensure a smooth continuation and to avoid repetition.

10 Summary and conclusions

The main conclusions of the report that have been discussed in section 8 should be summarized here briefly and simply. Only conclusions that can be justifiably drawn from the findings should be made. That sounds (and is) obvious, but there is often a great temptation to drop in an opinion for which no evidence is provided in the report. Take care or you may spoil a good report by including a throwaway remark.

Before you write this section, read through the whole report and make a note of key points. Readers who want a quick idea of what your research is about will look at the abstract, possibly the introduction and almost certainly at the summary and conclusions. This final section should be sufficiently succinct and clearly expressed to enable readers to understand quite clearly what research has been done and the conclusions that have been drawn *from the evidence*.

11 List of references

Opinions vary as to whether a full bibliography or a list of references, or both, should be included. My view is that only books and articles which have been cited or referred to in the report should be provided. However, some institutions also wish to have a bibliography which includes all sources consulted during the preparation of the investigation. You will need to consult your supervisor about institutional practice.

If you adopt the Harvard method of referencing, which I have recommended in this book, then references will appear in alphabetical order, which simplifies the process and avoids overlap. The amount of time it takes you to produce a bibliography, list of references, or both, will depend on how meticulous you were when you first recorded your sources. This is the time when hard work and systematic recording will really pay off.

12 Appendices

Copies of any research instruments (questionnaires, interview schedules, etc.) that have been used should be included in an appendix, unless you have been instructed otherwise. Your tutor will not wish to receive all completed questionnaires and would no doubt be dismayed if weighty parcels arrived on the doorstep, but one copy of any data-collecting instrument that has been used is generally required.

13 Length

Guidelines about length will be provided by your supervisor and many institutions will have rules about length. If you have not been told what length is expected, ask. If a maximum number of words is stipulated, stick to that number. You may be penalized for exceeding the limit.

14 Quotations

All quotations must be acknowledged. Remember that your tutor has probably read the same books, so is likely to recognize the source. If you are quoting only a few words or one sentence, it will be sufficient to indicate this by using inverted commas in the main text, with the source in brackets. If words are missed out of the quotation, indicate by three full stops. For example, as Hopkins (1985: 78) says, 'Documents . . . can illuminate rationale and purpose in interesting ways.' If the quotation is longer, indent it and (if the report is typed), use single spacing:
  As Hopkins says:

> Documents (memos, letters, position papers, examination papers, newspaper clippings, etc.) surrounding a curriculum or other educational concern can illuminate rationale and purpose in interesting ways. The use of such material can provide background information and understanding of issues that would not otherwise be available.
>
> (Hopkins 1985: 78)

15 Presentation

It is desirable, though not always essential for small-scale studies, that reports should by typed (check institutional rules). Typed copy should be in double spacing, and pages should be numbered.

Type or write on one side of the page only, leaving a left-hand margin of one and a half inches. Incidentally, if you are sending your report to be typed or are submitting a handwritten copy, make sure your writing is legible. It is not wise to annoy either your typist or your examiner by handing in an illegible scrawl.

If you are hopeless at typing and can afford to pay for your copy to be produced by a skilled typist, remember that it is not his or her job to correct spelling, punctuation, headings, grammar or wording. Do not expect your abbreviations to be interpreted, nor your additions to be checked. If is your job to hand in good, clear copy with very precise instructions about how things are to be done. If you make changes after the final copy is produced, you may have to pay more than you had bargained for, so take care.

The need for revision

Barzun and Graff (1977: 31) remind us that 'NO ONE, HOWEVER GIFTED, CAN PRODUCE A PASSABLE FIRST DRAFT. WRITING MEANS REWRITING.' You may find you need two, three or even more drafts before you are satisfied with the final result, so time must be set aside for this writing and refining process.

One problem about spending so much time on the original draft (the most difficult part of the writing stage) is that parts of it may seem right simply because they have been read so often. Another is that you may be so familiar with the subject that you assume something is understandable to the reader when it is not. Time will give you a better perspective on your writing, so you should put the script aside – for several days if you can – so that you can return to it with a more critical eye. This will help you to identify repetitive passages, errors of expression and lack of clarity.

Work through your first draft section by section to ensure its sense, accuracy, logical sequencing and soundness of expression. (If you wrote only one paragraph on one side of each sheet, as suggested, this correcting and reordering stage will be relatively straightforward.) In particular, check spelling (always have a dictionary to hand), quotations, punctuation, referencing, the overuse of certain terms (a *Roget's Thesaurus* can help you to find alternative forms of expression), and grammar (particularly consistency of tense).

Remind yourself as you read that whatever structure has been selected, your readers will wish to be quite clear why you carried out the investigation, how you conducted it, what methods you used to gather your evidence and what you found out. It is not enough to describe: you will be expected to analyse, to evaluate and, if the evidence merits it, to make recommendations.

If research findings are to be put into practice, they have to be presented in a way in which practitioners and policy-makers can understand them. Please bear this in mind when you present your projects. There is no special academic language that should be used in academic papers. Good, clear English remains good, clear English, whatever the context. Technical language may well save time when you are talking to colleagues with a similar background to your own, but it rarely translates well onto paper, and your readers (and your examiner) may become irritated by too much jargon or obscure language.

The need for revision and rewriting was emphasized in a recent radio interview, when a world-famous economist who had many scholarly books to his credit, was complimented by the interviewer on his style or writing. 'It must be a great advantage to you,' said the interviewer, 'to be able to write so freely and so easily. How do you do it?' The economist revealed his secret as follows:

> First I produce a draft and then I leave it alone for a day or two. Then I go back to it and decide that it has been written by an ignoramus, so I throw it away. Then I produce a second draft and leave it alone for a few days. I read it and decide there are the germs of a few good ideas there, but it is so badly written that it is not worth keeping, so I throw it away. After a few days, I write a third draft. I leave it alone for a while and when I read it again I discover that the ideas are developing, that there is some coherence to my arguments and that the grammar is not too bad. I correct this draft, change paragraphs around, insert new thoughts, remove overlapping passages and begin to feel quite pleased with myself. After a few

days, I read through this fourth draft, make final corrections and hand over the fifth draft to the typist. At this stage, I find I have usually achieved the degree of spontaneity for which I have been striving.

You may not need five drafts. Three may be enough if you write easily, but rest assured that no one gets away with one or two – and most of us take four or five.

When you have completed the writing to the best of your ability, try to enlist the help of someone who will read over the manuscript to look for remaining errors. Failing that, you could read your report out loud, though make sure you are alone or your family may feel the strain has been too much for you! Reading aloud is particularly useful for detecting the need for better linking passages.

Any possibility of plagiarism?

A word of warning. Take great care to ensure that you have not committed the sin of plagiarism. If you have been meticulous in recording sources, making it clear in your notes what are direct quotations, your paraphrasing or your own thoughts, then you will have no problems and there will be no possibility of accusations of sharp practice. Even so, take particular care to acknowledge sources, even if this means that you have to spend valuable time rechecking your records. Make sure you have followed the guidelines on plagiarism which I am confident your institution will have in place. The University of Manchester (1997: 1) defines plagiarism as 'the theft or expropriation of someone else's work without proper acknowledgement, presenting the material as if it were one's own', and warns that 'plagiarism is a serious academic offence and the consequences are severe'. The Australian Vice Chancellors' Committee (1990: 5) considers plagiarism to be 'the direct copying of textural material, the use of other people's data without acknowledgement and the use of ideas from other people without adequate attribution'.

Well, of course, you would not do any of those things, but there are other traps which at first may not occur to you. The University of Manchester (1997: 2) sternly warns that 'it is not acceptable for you to put together unacknowledged passages from the same or from different sources linking these together with a few words or sentences of your own and changing a few words from the original text: this is regarded as over-dependence on other sources, which is a form of plagiarism'.

There have been some unfortunate well-publicized plagiarism cases recently which have brought discredit to the individuals concerned and now supervisors are on the lookout for any examples in your draft. However, the final responsibility is yours, so take care. Guidelines are regularly updated, so make sure you have a copy of the latest version which in all probability will appear in your university or college programme handbooks and in any published codes of practice relating to academic standards.

Plagiarism has become an important issue in all research, essay and report writing, so make sure you are in the clear in every way.

Evaluating your own research

If you were writing a critique of a piece of research done by someone else, you would need to decide on criteria by which the research was to be judged. Verma and Beard (1981: 34–5) make the point that there is no universally accepted yardstick for judging research reports. The criteria will depend on the nature of the research. Sapsford and Evans (1984: 265) agree to an extent but they feel there are certain questions that should be asked of *any* piece of research. Both Verma and Beard, and Sapsford and Evans make suggestions about the types of questions to which answers might (or should) be sought. It is always a good idea to subject your own research to similarly rigorous examination before your script is handed over to the typist. Better that you should identify areas of weakness while there is time to correct them than leaving it to the examiner. The examiner just might decide your work is not up to scratch and so not worthy of a pass. So, before handing over what you hope will be your final draft, subject your own report to rigorous examination. Ask yourself:

1 Is the meaning clear? Are there any obscure passages?
2 Is the report well written? Check tenses, grammar, spelling, overlapping passages, punctuation, jargon.
3 Is the referencing well done? Are there any omissions?
4 Does the abstract give the reader a clear idea of what is in the report?
5 Does the title indicate the nature of the study?
6 Are the objectives of the study stated clearly?
7 Are the objectives fulfilled?
8 If hypotheses were postulated, are they proved or not proved?
9 Has a sufficient amount of literature relating to the topic been studied?
10 Does the literature review, if any, provide an indication of the state of knowledge in the subject? Is your topic placed in the context of the area of study as a whole?
11 Are all terms clearly defined?
12 Are the selected methods of data collection accurately described? Are they suitable for the task? Why were they chosen?
13 Are any limitations of the study clearly presented?
14 Have any statistical techniques been used? If so, are they appropriate for the task?
15 Are the data analysed and interpreted or merely described?
16 Are the results clearly presented? Are tables, diagrams and figures well drawn?
17 Are conclusions based on evidence? Have any claims been made that cannot be substantiated?
18 Is there any evidence of bias? Any emotive terms or intemperate language?
19 Are the data likely to be reliable? Could another researcher repeat the methods used and have a reasonable chance of getting the same or similar results?
20 Are recommendations (if any) feasible?
21 Are there any unnecessary items in the appendix?
22 Would you give the report a passing grade if you were the examiner? If not, perhaps an overhaul is necessary.

Once you have satisfied yourself that you have been able to answer all these questions to your satisfaction, you will be ready to produce the final draft. Check the final, typed copy. Even expert typists can make mistakes and, if your writing is bad, it is inevitable that mistakes will be made.

Finally, congratulate yourself on an excellent job completed on time. Hand in your report and give yourself an evening off!

⊙ Writing the report checklist

1	Set deadlines.	Allocate dates for sessions, sub-sections and the whole report. Keep an eye on your schedule.
2	Write regularly.	
3	Create a rhythm of work.	Don't stop to check references. Make a note of what has to be checked, but don't stop.
4	Write up a section as soon as it is ready.	Try particularly to produce a draft of the literature review as soon as the bulk of your reading is completed.
5	Stop at a point from which it is easy to resume writing.	
6	Leave space for revisions.	Use one side of the page only. Try to keep to one paragraph per page.
7	Publicize your plans.	You may need a little help from your friends to meet the deadlines.
8	Check that all essential sections have been covered.	Abstract, outline of the research, review of previous work, statement of the scope and aims of the investigation, description of procedures, statement of results, discussion, summary and conclusions, references.
9	Check length is according to institutional requirements.	You don't want to be failed on a technicality.
10	Don't forget the title page.	

11 Any acknowledgements
    and thanks?

12 Include headings where
    possible.

Anything to make it easier for
readers to follow the structure will
help.

13 Number tables and figures
    and provide titles.

Check tables and figures for
accuracy, particularly after typing.

14 Make sure all quotations
    are acknowledged.

Check that quotations are
presented in a consistent format.

15 Provide a list of references.

Unless instructed otherwise,
include only items to which
reference is made in the report.
Check that a consistent system is
used and that there are no
omissions.

16 Appendices should only
    include items that are
    required for reference
    purposes. Do not clutter
    the report with
    irrelevant items.

Unless instructed otherwise, one
copy of each data-collecting
instrument should be included.

17 Remember to leave
    sufficient time for revision
    and rewriting.

Check that you have written in
plain English. Check that your
writing is legible.

18 Try to get someone to
    read the report.

Fresh eyes will often see errors
you have overlooked.

POSTSCRIPT

There may be occasions when, in spite of careful planning and preparation, a project does not go according to plan. You may find that people who said they were willing to provide information by a certain date fail to do so, for example, or that results were not forthcoming. If things do go wrong, consult your tutor to discuss the best course of action. You may have learnt a great deal about conducting an investigation and the topic you were investigating, even though the outcome may not be what you had hoped. If you are not able to produce a report on the lines you planned, you may be able to submit a report of what you have been able to do, together with an account of what went wrong and why and, if appropriate, how you would have planned and carried out the investigation if you were starting again. The important thing is to ask for help. Intelligent people who are first-time researchers sometimes feel they ought to be able to sort themselves out, and by not making use of supervisors, computer-centre staff and librarians, may waste a great deal of time. I said in the Introduction to this book that we all learn how to do research by actually doing it. That is quite true, but anyone carrying out an investigation for the first time needs some assistance. Make sure you take advantage of any that is available.

Just one final word. People who agree to be interviewed or to complete questionnaires, diary forms or checklists, groups who agree to your observing meetings, and keepers of archives who allow you to consult documents, deserve consideration and thanks. Daphne Johnson sums up the position well:

> If files are left in disarray, papers borrowed and not returned, or respondents subjected to too lengthy or frequent interviews, at inconvenient times, the researcher's welcome will be worn out. All social researchers are to some extent mendicants, since they are seeking a free gift of time or information from those who are the subject of study. But researchers who bear this fact in mind, and who, without becoming the captive of their respondents, can contrive to make the research experience a helpful and profitable one, will almost certainly be gratified by the generosity with which people will give their time and knowledge.
>
> (Johnson 1984: 11)

REFERENCES

Adelman, C., Jenkins, D. and Kemmis, S. (1977) 'Re-thinking case study: notes from the second Cambridge conference', *Cambridge Journal of Education*, 6, 139–50.

Atkinson, P. and Delamont, S. (1985) 'A critique of "case study" research in education' in Shipman, M. (ed.) *Educational Research Principles, Policies and Practices*. Lewes: Falmer Press.

Australian Vice Chancellors' Committee (1990) *Guidelines for Responsible Practice in Research and Dealing with Problems of Research Misconduct*. Deakin, Victoria: Australian Vice Chancellors' Committee.

Baker, S. and Carty, J. (1994) 'Literature searching: finding, organizing and recording information', Chapter 15 in Bennett, N., Glatter, R. and Levačić, R. (eds) *Improving Education Management through Research and Consultancy*. London: Paul Chapman, in association with The Open University.

Bales, R.F. (1950) *Interaction Process Analysis: A Method for the Study of Small Groups*. Cambridge, MA: Addison-Wesley.

Barnett, V.D. and Lewis, T. (1963) 'A study of the relation between GCE and degree results', *Journal of the Royal Statistical Society*, A(126), 187–226.

Barnett, V.D., Holder, R.L. and Lewis, T. (1968) 'Some new results on the association between students' ages and their degree results', *Journal of the Royal Statistical Society*, A(131).

Bartholomew, J. (1971) 'The teacher as researcher', *Hard Cheese*, 1.

Barzun, J. and Graff, H.E. (1977) *The Modern Researcher*, 3rd edn. New York: Harcourt Brace Jovanovich.

Bassey, M. (1981) 'Pedagogic research: on the relative merits of the search for generalization and study of single events', *Oxford Review of Education*, 7(1), 73–93.

Bell, J. (1996) 'An investigation into barriers to completion of postgraduate research degrees in three universities'. Unpublished report funded through the Leverhulme Emeritus research fund.

Bell, J., Bush, T., Fox, A. *et al.* (eds) (1984) *Conducting Small-scale Investigations in Educational Management*. London: Harper & Row.

Berger, R.M. and Patchner, M.A. (1994) 'Research ethics', Chapter 6 in Bennett, N., Glatter, R. and Levačić, R. (eds) (1994) *Improving Educational Management through Research and Consultancy*. London: Paul Chapman, in association with The Open University.

Best, J.W. (1970) *Research in Education*, 2nd edn. New Jersey: Prentice-Hall.

Blaxter, L., Dodd, K. and Tight, M. (1996a) 'Mature student markets: an institutional case study', *Higher Education*, 31(2), 187–203.

Blaxter, L., Hughes, C. and Tight, M. (1996b) *How to Research*. Buckingham: Open University Press.

Boehm, A.E. and Weinberg, R.A. (1977) *The Classroom Observer: A Guide for Developing Observation Skills*. New York: Teachers' College Press.

Bogdan, R.C. and Biklen, S.K. (1982) *Qualitative Research for Education: An Introduction to Theory and Methods*. Boston, MA: Allyn & Bacon.

Bogdan, R.C. and Taylor, S.J. (1975) *Introduction to Qualitative Research Methods*. London: Wiley.

Borg, W.R. (1981) *Applying Educational Research: A Practical Guide for Teachers*. New York: Longman.

Bradley, H.W. and Eggleston, J.F. (1976) *An Induction Year Experiment*. Report of an experiment carried out by Derbyshire, Lincolnshire and Nottinghamshire LEAs and the University of Nottingham School of Education.

Brenner, M., Brown, J. and Canter, D. (1985) *The Research Interview: Uses and Approaches*. New York: Academic Press.

Bromley, D.B. (1986) *The Case Study Method in Psychology and Related Disciplines*. Chichester: John Wiley.

Brown, S. and McIntyre, D. (1981) 'An action-research approach to innovation in centralized educational systems', *European Journal of Science Education*, 3(3), 243–58.

Bryman, A. and Cramer, D. (1990) *Quantitative Data Analysis for Social Scientists*. London: Routledge.

Burgess, R.G. (1981) 'Keeping a research diary', *Cambridge Journal of Education*, 11, pt 1, 75–83.

Burgess, R.G. (1982) 'The unstructured interview as conversation' in Burgess, R.G. (ed.) *Field Research: A Source Book and Field Manual*. London: Allen & Unwin.

Burgess, R.G. (1994) 'On diaries and diary keeping', Chapter 21 in Bennett *et al. Improving Educational Management through Research and Consultancy*. London: Paul Chapman.

Carr, W. and Kemmis, S. (1986) *Becoming Critical: Education, Knowledge and Action Research*. Lewes: Falmer Press.

Casey, K. (1993) 'The new narrative research in education', *Review of Research in Education*, 21, 211–53.

Cohen, L. (1976) *Educational Research in Classrooms and Schools: A Manual of Materials and Methods*. London: Harper & Row.

Cohen, L. and Manion, L. (1994) *Research Methods in Education*, 4th edn. London: Routledge.

Coolican, H. (1994) *Research Methods and Statistics in Psychology*, 2nd edn. London: Hodder and Stoughton.

Cope, E. and Gray, J. (1979) 'Teachers as researchers: some experience of an alternative paradigm', *British Educational Research Journal*, 5(2), 237–51.

Cross, K.P. (1981) *Adults as Learners: Increasing Participation and Facilitating Learning*. San Francisco: Jossey-Bass.

Delamont, S., Atkinson, P. and Parry, O. (1997) *Supervising the PhD: A Guide to Success*. Buckingham: SRHE and Open University Press.

Denscombe, M. (1998) *The Good Research Guide*. Buckingham: Open University Press.

Derbyshire Education Committee (1966) 'Awards to students' (mimeo).

Dixon, B.R., Bouma, G.D. and Atkinson, G.B.J. (1987) *A Handbook of Social Science Research*. Oxford: Oxford University Press.

Drew, C.J. (1980) *Introduction to Designing and Conducting Research*, 2nd edn. Missouri: C.B. Mosby Company.

Duffy, B. (1998) 'Late nineteenth-century popular educational conservatism: the work of coalminers on the school boards of the North-East', *History of Education*, 27(1), 29–38.

Eaton, E.G. (1980) 'The academic performance of mature age students: a review of the general literature' in Hore, T. and West, L.H.T. (eds) *Mature Age Students in Australian Higher Education*. Higher Education Advisory and Research Unit, Monash University, Australia.

Eggleston, J. (1979) 'The characteristics of educational research: mapping the domain', *British Educational Research Journal*, 5(1), 1–12.

Elliott, J. (1991) *Action Research for Educational Change*. Buckingham: Open University Press.

Elton, G.R. (1967) *The Practice of History*. London: Fontana Library.

Evans, R.J. (1997) *In Defence of History*. London: Granta Books.

Fagin, M.C. (1971) *Life Experience has Academic Value*. ERIC Document Reproduction Service, ED04 7219.

Fidler, B. (1992) 'Telephone interviewing', reprinted as Chapter 19 in

Bennett, N., Glatter, R. and Levačić, R. (eds) (1994) *Improving Educational Management through Research and Consultancy*. London: Paul Chapman, in association with The Open University.

Flanagan, J.C. (1951) 'Defining the requirements of the executive's job', *Personnel*, 28, 28–35.

Flanagan, J.C. (1954) 'The critical incident technique', *Psychological Bulletin*, 51, 327–58.

Flanders, N.A. (1970) *Analysing Teaching Behaviour*. Cambridge, MA: Addison-Wesley.

Flecker, R. (1959) 'Characteristics of passing and failing students in first-year university mathematics', *The Educand*, 3(3).

Fleming, W.G. (1959) *Personal and Academic Factors as Predictors of First-year Success in Ontario Universities*. Atkinson Study Report No. 5, University of Toronto, Department of Educational Research.

Frank, F. and Houghton, G. (1997) 'When life gets in the way', *Adults Learning*, May, 244–5.

Galton, M. (1978) *British Mirrors*. Leicester: University of Leicester School of Education.

Gavron, H. (1996) *The Captive Wife*. London: Routledge & Kegan Paul.

Glatter, R. (1997) 'Context and capability in educational management', *Educational Management and Administration*, 25(2), 181–92.

Goulding, S. (1984) 'Analysis and presentation of information', Chapter 11 in Bell, J., Bush, T. and Fox, A. *et al. Conducting Small-scale Investigations in Educational Management*. London: Harper & Row.

Gray, J. (1998) 'Narrative Inquiry'. Unpublished paper, Edith Cowan University, Western Australia.

Great Britain Training Agency (1989) *Training in Britain: Individuals' Perspectives*. Sheffield: Training Agency.

Grebenik, E. and Moser, C.A. (1962) 'Society: problems and methods of study' in Welford, A.T., Argyle, M., Glass, O. and Morris, J.N. (eds) *Statistical Surveys*. London: Routledge & Kegan Paul.

Gudmunsdottir, S. (1996) 'The teller, the tale, and the one being told: the narrative nature of the research interview', *Curriculum Inquiry*, 26(3), 293–306.

Hakim, C. (1982) *Secondary Analysis in Social Research: A Guide to Data Sources and Methods with Examples*. London: Allen & Unwin.

Hammersley, M. (1987) 'Some notes on the terms "validity" and "reliability" ', *British Educational Research Journal*, 13(1), 73–81.

Hammersley, M. (1990) *Classroom Ethnography: Empirical and Methodological Essays*. Buckingham: Open University Press.

Hammersley, M. and Atkinson, P. (1983) *Ethnography: Principles in Practice*. London: Tavistock.

Harris, D. (1940) 'Factors affecting college grades: a review of the literature', *Psychology Bulletin*, 37.

Hart, E. and Bond, M. (1995) *Action Research for Health and Social Care: A Guide to Practitioners*. Buckingham: Open University Press.

Haywood, P. and Wragg, E.C. (1982) *Evaluating the Literature*. Rediguide 2, University of Nottingham School of Education.

Holly, M.L. (1984) *Keeping a Personal Professional Journal*. Deakin, Melbourne: Deakin University Press.

Holsti, O.R. (1969) *Content Analysis for the Social Sciences and Humanities*. Reading, MA: Addison-Wesley.

Hopkins, D. (1985) *A Teacher's Guide to Classroom Research*. Milton Keynes: Open University Press.

Howard, K. and Sharp, J.A. (1983) *The Management of a Student Research Project*. Aldershot: Gower.

Howell, D.A. (1962) *A Study of the 1955 Entry to British Universities*. Evidence to the Robbins Committee on Higher Education. University of London (mimeo).

Johnson, D. (1984) 'Planning small-scale research' in Bell, J., Bush, T. and Fox, A. *et al. Conducting Small-scale Investigations in Educational Management*. London: Harper & Row.

Kapur, K.L. (1972) 'Student wastage at Edinburgh University: factors related to failure and drop-out', *Universities Quarterly*, Summer.

Karkalas, A.M. and MacKenzie, A. (undated) 'Report of reasons for non-completion of the Department of Adult and Continuing Education university introduction to study for mature students during three years'. University of Glasgow: Department of Adult and Continuing Education.

Kinnear, P.R. and Gray, C.D. (1994) *SPSS for Windows Made Simple*. Hove: Laurence Erlbaum.

Kirk, J. and Miller, M.L. (1985) *Reliability and Validity in Qualitative Research*. Newbury Park, CA: Sage.

Kitson Clark, G. (1967) *The Critical Historian*. London: Heinemann.

Krippendorff, K. (1980) *Content Analysis*. London: Sage.

Lacey, C. (1976) 'Problems of sociological fieldwork: a review of the methodology of "Hightown Grammar"' in Shipman, M. (ed.) *The Organisation and Impact of Social Research*. London: Routledge & Kegan Paul.

Langeveld, M.J. (1965) 'In search of research' in *Paedagogica Europoea: The European Year Book of Educational Research*, Vol. 1. Amsterdam: Elsevier.

Lehmann, I.J. and Mehrens, W.A. (1971) *Educational Research*. New York: Holt, Rinehart & Winston.

McCracken, D. (1969) *University Student Performance*. Report of the Student Health Department, University of Leeds.

McGivney, V. (1996a) *Staying or Leaving the Course: Non-completion and Retention of Mature Students in Further and Higher Education*. Leicester: National Institute of Adult Continuing Education.

McGivney, V. (1996b) 'Staying or leaving the course: non-completion and retention', *Adults Learning*, February, 133–5.

McIntosh, N. and Woodley, A. (1975) 'Excellence, equality and the open university'. Paper presented to the working party on Teaching and Learning and the New Media, 3rd International Conference on Higher Education, United Kingdom, University of Lancaster.

McNiff, J. (1988) *Action Research: Principles and Practice*. Basingstoke: Macmillan Education.

Malleson, N.B. (1959) 'University student, 1953', I-profile, *Universities Quarterly*, 13, 287–98.

Marples, D.L. (1967) 'Studies of managers: a fresh start', *Journal of Management Studies*, 4, 282–99.

Marsh, C. (1982) *The Survey Method: The Contribution of Surveys to Sociological Explanation*. London: Allen & Unwin.

Marsh, C. (1988) *Exploring Data: An Introduction to Data Analysis for Social Sciences*. London: Polity Press.

Marwick, A. (1989) *The Nature of History*, 3rd edn. London: Macmillan.

May, T. (1993) *Social Research: Issues, Methods and Process*. Buckingham: Open University Press.

Medawar, P.B. (1972) *The Hope of Progress*. London: Methuen.

Moser, C.A. and Kalton, G. (1971) *Survey Methods in Social Investigation*, 2nd edn. London: Heinemann.

Mountford, Sir J. (1957) *How they Fared: A Survey of a Three-year Student Entry*. Liverpool: Liverpool University Press.

Nai, C. (1996) 'Stretching the aged workforce: a study of the barriers to continuous learning among mature workers'. Unpublished dissertation submitted in part requirement for the degree of Master of Education (Training and Development) at the University of Sheffield.

Nisbet, J.D. (1977) 'Small-scale research: guidelines and suggestions for development', *Scottish Educational Studies*, 9, May, 13–17.

Nisbet, J.D. and Entwistle, N.J. (1970) *Educational Research Methods*. London: University of London Press.

Nisbet, J.D. and Watt, J. (1980) *Case Study*. Rediguide 26, University of Nottingham School of Education.

Open University course D101 (1988) *Technology Foundation Course*. Milton Keynes, Open University Educational Enterprises.

Open University course E111 (1988) *Educational Evaluation*. Milton Keynes, Open University Educational Enterprises.

Oppenheim, A.N. (1966) *Questionnaire Design and Attitude Measurement*. London: Heinemann.

Orna, E. with Stevens, G. (1995) *Managing Information for Research*. Buckingham: Open University Press.

Oxtoby, R. (1979) 'Problems facing heads of department', *Journal of Further and Higher Education*, 3(1), Spring, 46–59.

Peberdy, A. (1993) 'Observing', Chapter 4 in Shakespeare, P., Atkinson, D. and French, F. (eds) *Reflecting on Research Practice: Issues in Health Care and Social Welfare*. Buckingham: Open University Press.

Peeke, G. (1984) 'Teacher as researcher', *Educational Research*, 26(1), February, 24–6.

Philips, H. and Cullen, A. (1955) 'Age and academic success', *Forum of Education*, 14.

Phillips, E.M. and Pugh, D.S. (1987) *How to Get a PhD: Managing the Peaks and Troughs of Research*. Milton Keynes: Open University Press.

Platt, J. (1981) 'On interviewing one's peers', *British Journal of Sociology*, 32(1), March, 75–91.

Powney, J. and Watts, M. (1987) *Interviewing in Educational Research*. London: Routledge & Kegan Paul.

Preedy, M. and Riches, C. (1985) 'A methodological analysis of some research reports by practitioners on teacher–parent communications', for the Open University course *Applied Studies in Educational Management* (EP851), The Open University, School of Education (paper presented to the BEMAS Conference 'Research and Administration in Secondary Education', Nov. 1985).

Raven, M. and Parker, F. (1981) 'Research in education and the in-service student', *British Journal of In-service Education*, 8(1), Autumn, 42–4.

Richardson, E. (1973) *The Teacher, the School and the Task of Management*. London: Heinemann.

Ruyle, J. and Geiselman, L.A. (1974) 'Non-traditional opportunities and programs' in Cross, K.P. and Valley, J.R. (eds) *Planning Non-traditional Programs: An Analysis of the Issues for Postsecondary Education*. San Francisco: Jossey-Bass.

Sanders, C. (1961) *Psychological and Educational Bases of Academic Performance*. Brisbane: Australian Council for Educational Research.

Sanders, C. (1963) 'Australian universities and their educational problems', *The Australian University*, 1, 2.

Sapsford, R.J. and Evans, J. (1984) 'Evaluating a research report' in Bell, J., Bush, T. and Fox, A. *et al.* (eds) *Conducting Small-scale Investigations in Educational Management*. London: Harper & Row. Adapted from material prepared for Open University course DE304, *Research Methods in the Social Sciences* (1979), Block 8, Part 1, pp. 9–22.

Scott, C. (1961) 'Research on mail surveys', *Journal of the Royal Statistical Society*, Series A (124), 143–205.

Scott, C., Burns, A. and Cooney, G. (1996) 'Reasons for discontinuing study: the case of mature age female students with children', *Higher Education*, 31(2), March, 233–53.

Selltiz, D., Jahoda, M., Deutsch, M. and Cook, S.W. (1962) *Research Methods in Social Relations*, 2nd edn. New York: Holt, Rinehart & Winston.

Sharon, A.T. (1971) 'Adult academic achievement in relation to formal education and age', *Adult Education Journal*, 21.

Shaw, K.E. (1975) 'Negotiating curriculum change in a college of education' in Reid, W.A. and Walker, D.F. (eds) *Case Studies in Curriculum Change*. London: Routledge & Kegan Paul.

Shaw, K.E. (1978) *Researching an Organization*. Rediguide 24. University of Nottingham School of Education.

Simon, A. and Boyer, E. (1975) *The Reflective Practitioner*. New York: Basic Books.

Simons, H. (1984) 'Ethical principles in school self-evaluation' in Bell, J., Bush, T. and Fox, A. *et al.* (eds) *Conducting Small-scale Investigations in Educational Management*. London: Harper & Row.

Small, J.J. (1966) *Achievement and Adjustment in the First Year at University*. Wellington: New Zealand Council for Educational Research.

Spradley, J.P. (1980) *Participant Observation*. New York: Holt, Rinehart & Winston.

SPSS (1990) *SPSS User's Guide*. Chicago: SPSS Inc.

SPSS (1990) *SPSS Categories*. Chicago: SPSS Inc.

Stanford, M. (1994) *A Companion to the Study of History*. Oxford: Blackwell.

Strauss, A. (1987) *Qualitative Analysis for Social Scientists*. Cambridge: Cambridge University Press.

Thody, A. with Downes, P., Hewlett, M. and Tomlinson, H. (1997) 'Lies, damned lies – and storytelling: an exploration of the contribution of principals' anecdotes to research, teaching and learning about the management of schools and colleges', *Educational Management and Administration*, 25(3), July, 325–38.

Thomas, W., Beeby, C.E. and Oram, M.H. (1939) *Entrance to the University*. Wellington: New Zealand Council for Educational Research.

Tosh, J. (1991) *The Pursuit of History*, 2nd edn. Harlow: Longman.

UMIST (University of Manchester Institute of Science and Technology) Graduate School (1998) 'Code of practice on the admission, supervision and examination of research students: appeals procedures for research degrees' (mimeo).

University of Manchester (1997) 'Plagiarism' (mimeo).

Verma, G.K. and Beard, R.M. (1981) *What is Educational Research? Perspectives on Techniques of Research*. Aldershot: Gower.

Vyas, H. (1979) 'The teacher as researcher', *Educational Review*, 11(3), Summer, 58–64.

Walker, P. (1975) 'The university performance of mature students', *Research in Education*, 14, 1–13.

Weber, R.P. (1990) *Basic Content Analysis*. Newbury Park, CA: Sage.

Williams, G.L. (1984) *Making Your Meetings More Interesting and Effective*. Sheffield City Polytechnic: Pavid Publications.

Williams, G.L. (1994) 'Observing and recording meetings', Chapter 22 in Bennett, N., Glatter, R. and Levačić, R. *Improving Educational Management through Research and Consultancy*. London: Paul Chapman, in association with The Open University.

Wilson, N.J. (1979) 'The ethnographic style of research' in Block 1 (Variety in Social Science Research), Part I (Styles of Research) of Open University course DE304, *Research Methods in Education and the Social Sciences*.

Winter, R. (1987) *Action Research and the Nature of Social Inquiry: Professional Innovation and Educational Work*. Aldershot: Avebury.

Wiseman, J.P. and Aron, M.S. (1972) *Field Reports in Sociology*. London: Transworld Publishers.

Woodley, A. (1979) 'The prediction of degree performance among undergraduates in the commerce and social science faculty', University of Birmingham (unpublished).

Woodley, A. (1985) 'Taking account of mature students' in Jacques, D. and Richardson, J. (eds) *The Future of Higher Education*. Guildford: SRHE and NFER-Nelson.

Woodley, A. (1998) *Review of McGivney (1996a) 'Staying or Leaving the Course; Non-completion and Retention of Mature Students in Further and Higher Education'*. Leicester: National Institute of Adult Continuing Education.

Wragg, E.C. (1980) *Conducting and Analysing Interviews*. Rediguide 11. University of Nottingham School of Education.

Wragg, E.C. and Kerry, T.L. (1978) *Classroom Interaction Research*. Rediguide 14. University of Nottingham School of Education. Also reproduced as Chapter 11 in Bell, J., Bush, T. and Fox, A. *et al.* (eds) (1984) *Conducting Small-scale Investigations in Educational Management*. London: Harper & Row, and as Chapter 18 in Bennett, N., Glatter, R. and Levačić, R. (eds) (1994) *Improving Educational Management through Research and Consultancy*. London: Paul Chapman, in association with The Open University.

Yin, R. (1993) *Applications of Case Study Research*. Newbury Park, CA: Sage.

Yin, R.K. (1994) Designing single- and multiple-case studies, in Bennett,

N., Glatter, R. and Levačić, R. (eds) *Improving Educational Management through Research and Consultancy*. London: Paul Chapman.

Youngman, M.B. (1982) *Designing and Analysing Questionnaires*. Rediguide 12. University of Nottingham School of Education. An updated version appears as Chapter 17, 'Designing and using questionnaires' in Bennett, N., Glatter, R. and Levačić, R. (eds) (1994) *Improving Educational Management through Research and Consultancy*. London: Paul Chapman, in association with The Open University.

Youngman, M.B. (1986) Analysing Questionnaires. Nottingham: University of Nottingham School of Education.

Zimmerman, D.H. and Wieder, D.L. (1977) 'The diary-interview method', *Urban Life*, 5(4), January, 479–99.

INDEX

WRITING AT UNIVERSITY
A GUIDE FOR STUDENTS

Phyllis Creme and Mary R. Lea

- As a student, what do you need to do to tackle writing assignments at university?
- How can you write more confidently and effectively?
- How can you address the variety of written assignments that you encounter in your studies?

Writing at University will make you more aware of the complexity of the writing process. It provides useful strategies and approaches that will allow you to gain more control over your own academic writing. You are encouraged to build upon your existing abilities as a writer and to develop your writing in academic settings through applying a series of practical tasks to your own work. The complete process of writing assignments is considered, including attention to disciplinary diversity, the relationship between reading and writing, the use of personal, and textual cohesion.

This book is an essential tool to help you develop an awareness and understanding of what it means to be a successful student writer in higher education today.

It will also be invaluable to academic staff who want to support students with their writing.

Contents
You and your university writing – First thoughts on writing assignments – Writing for different courses – Beginning with the title – Reading as part of writing – Organizing and shaping your writing – Writing your knowledge in an academic way – Putting it together – Completing the assignment and preparing for next time – References – Index.

160pp   0 335 19642 X (Paperback)   0 335 19643 8 (Hardback)

HOW TO GET A GOOD DEGREE
MAKING THE MOST OF YOUR TIME AT
UNIVERSITY

Phil Race

This book is designed to help students who are
aiming high. A good degree is a passport to a
better life. It opens up more choices regarding
career and employment. It brings you the possibility of better earnings. More than anything else, a good degree
brings freedom to choose, to change direction, and to follow up
interesting options. A good degree brings recognition and gets you
to the top of shortlists. Even if you go on to get higher degrees,
people will still look at whether your first degree was a good one or
not.

So how do you get a good degree? Is it all a matter of luck? Is it hard
work? In this book, you will find ways you can use to work systematically towards a good degree. There are no short-cuts regarding
working hard, but there are short-cuts about making sure the hard
work you do is the *right* hard work. Don't just read this book, however, *do it*! Have a go at each of the tasks in the book, and gain control of how you learn, so that you can fine-tune your learning to
achieve the success you are aiming for.

Contents
*Introduction: don't just work hard, work smart! – What is a good degree
really a measure of? – Capitalizing on teaching-learning situations –
Going for gold in assessed coursework – Putting your resources to work –
Aiming high in revision and exams – Looking after yourself – Final action
plan – References and further reading – Index.*

272pp   0 335 20024 9 (Paperback)   0 335 20025 7 (Hardback)

READING, WRITING AND REASONING
(2nd edition)
A GUIDE FOR STUDENTS

Gavin Fairbairn and Christopher Winch

Review of the first edition

The book's title is absolutely accurate in describing how the authors give the most practical and clear advice on all of the problematic aspects of reading for meaning, developing analytic and coherent thinking and writing in coursework.

This book will be invaluable for any student and it would be sad if most are too busy writing essays and undertaking examinations to read it.

Nursing Times

If you find writing essays difficult and leave them to the last minute, if you panic as the deadline for submission approaches then this is the book for you. This guide will enable you to develop essential skills in reading, writing and reasoning. The authors are both very experienced in helping students to develop proficiency in these areas. Written in plain language, the book encourages the development of skills in reading and evaluating texts, in the use of a clear and effective writing style and in cogent argument. The practical advice, examples and exercises are invaluable for all students who would like to become better readers, writers and reasoners.

Contents
Part 1: Reading, writing and talking – Talking and writing – What reading involves – What writing involves – Part 2: Writing as a student – Approaches to writing – Technical aspects of writing – Attending to style – Part 3: Developing coherent trains of thought – Influencing the beliefs of others – Arguments of different kinds – Analysing and evaluating arguments – Postscript – References – Index.

256pp   0 335 19740 X (Paperback)   0 335 19741 8 (Hardback)

A GUIDE TO LEARNING INDEPENDENTLY
THIRD EDITION

Lorraine Marshall and Frances Rowland

This new edition of *A Guide to Learning Independently* will take you into the twenty-first century. It will empower you to develop the necessary skills to survive as an informed, independent, and versatile student. The book will help you to:

- Understand yourself and the ways in which you learn and study
- Plan and concentrate on your study commitments
- Adapt to independent study within a formal institution such as a university
- Formulate effective strategies for remembering information
- Use and evaluate research material
- Make the most of libraries and other sources of information available to the contemporary student
- Understand and make the best use of lectures
- Participate confidently in discussion groups
- Develop, improve and succeed in your writing.

A Guide to Learning Independently will change the way you think about learning, and it will transform the ways in which you learn and study.

Contents
Read this first! – You – Planning when and how you study – Becoming an independent student – Asking your own questions – Learning and remembering – Choosing and analysing a topic – Researching a topic – Using libraries and other information sources – Reading – Listening to lectures – Participating in discussion groups – Developing your writing – Writing essays – Writing scientific reports – Using conventions – Learning from evaluation – Appendix: Discrimination – Sexist language and attitudes – Quotation sources – Reference books – Index.

312pp   0 335 20366 3 (Paperback)